THE 4 DEGREES
OF RELATIONSHIP

THE 4 DEGREES OF RELATIONSHIP

Friends: Choose Godly, Choose Wisely

DR. VICTOR T. NYARKO

gatekeeper press

Columbus, Ohio

The 4 Degrees of Relationship: Friends:
Choose Godly, Choose Wisely

Published by Gatekeeper Press
2167 Stringtown Rd, Suite 109
Columbus, OH 43123-2989
www.GatekeeperPress.com

ISBN: 9781642371093
eISBN: 9781642371086

Printed in the United States of America

Presented To

____

From

____

____

Date

____

Other Exciting Books by the Author.

DIVINE EMPOWERMENT

THIS BOOK IS an exposition on the power of the efficacious blood of Jesus Christ, the legacy and empowerment it provided for the first Apostles, for today's believer in Jesus Christ and for all who will come after. It reveals the resources that God, through Christ, has made available and at our disposal for the successful accomplishment of the great commission. It also teaches the reader how to tap into these resources by believing it, claiming it and possessing it.

ISBN978-14848

A DISCONNECTED GENERATION

THIS BOOK PRESENTS striking differences between the generation of Moses and the generation of Joshua. Although Joshua's generation witnessed a glimpse of the miracles and wonderful workings of God, they lacked a personal relationship with the God of their fathers and the God of Israel.

ISBN 1-59330-075-1

DEALING WITH REJECTION

REJECTION OF ONE kind or another is inevitable throughout ones' life, therefore any tool that can be acquired to help deal with it should be a welcome choice. In this book, Dr. Nyarko presents the key elements that lead to the feeling of rejection and how to deal with rejection from a biblical perspective.

ISBN 1-59330-471-4

BEAUTY FOR ASHES

IT HAS BEEN the church's tradition to think that a great revival could be sparked by extensive advertising, putting up the right preacher and playing the right music. If these are true ingredients for revival, then John the Baptist' revival, which ignited and blazed a trail in the desolate and obscure wilderness of Judea, wouldn't have had the impact it did. On the contrary, out of the ashes of repentance comes revival, refreshing restitution and restoration.

ISBN 1-59330-605-9

WHERE ARE THE FATHERS

THE LACK OF fathers at home has been one of society's greatest dilemmas of our time. This book has a timely word from the Lord for everyone. God our father is calling all fathers through the pen of this godly author and father, back to the honorable and critical role of fatherhood. Get ready, read it, repent and pass it on.

ISBN 13: 9781593302436

KINGDOM WORSHIP

MUSIC IS PART of worship, but good music alone does not constitute worship. In this book, the various Hebrew words for "praise" are described. It sheds light on the true meaning of worship and what the popular command "Hallelujah" means in the praise and worship of God. It comes from the two Hebrew words *Halal*, which is the most radical form of praise, and *Yah* which is the short form for Jehovah. Worshiping God goes far beyond being an act. It should be a personal encounter with God's presence which should lead to the worshipper leaving His presence with fulfillment and gratification. In brief, this book focuses on what it means to halal (praise) God, who ought to Halal (praise) Him and where he ought to be Halal (praise).

ISBN 978-1-4984-3509-3

THE PRODIGAL FATHER

What has become popularly but also erroneously referred to as the story of the "prodigal son" is part of a larger revelation that Jesus wanted to show his church. This book then culminates with the distinction that our Lord Jesus makes between Sonship and servanthood in his vineyard parable about the servants and sons who were sent out by the Lord to work on his vineyard. Are all humanity Sons of God through procreation, as many claim? Or, is there a distinction between Kingdom-Sons and Kingdom-Servants of God? This book's approach to the story will leave you amused, instructed, enlightened, stirred up, and challenged, but definitely not bored!

ISBN: 978-1-947349-23-0

THE ORDER OF MELCHIZEDEK.

This book takes the reader on an intriguing and interesting journey into the life and person of a strange and isolated but unique bible personage called Melchizedek, He appears momentarily on the scene of bible history with the great Patriarch Abraham and then disappears from the pages of history just as suddenly as he appeared. All other references in the bible about him are traced back to this one occasion. He is said to be without father, mother, or descent, having neither beginning of days, nor end of life. So, the questions is, who was Melchizedek? In what ways does his priestly order align with the Lord Jesus and yet differ from the Aaronic order of Priesthood? Why should Melchizedek, and he alone, of all the Old Testament characters be thought of in a way that defies human mortality? This book's approach to the life and person of Melchizedek will leave you amused, instructed, enlightened, stirred up, and challenged, but definitely not bored!

ISBN: 978-1-947349-21-6

DEDICATION

To Bishop Arthur & Lady Evan Thomas (USA)

&

The late Rev. Dr. (MD) Daniel & Regina Antwi (Ghana)

My Mentors in the ministry. You made indelible impressions on my ministry as no other mortal beings had done. May your efforts and labor of love be eternally rewarded.

&

To the Purity Movement.
The visionary—Joan Richards Nyarko, and to all the young men and women in Victory Family and other churches who have set themselves aside to live pure in a polluted world. It is your godly ambition that challenged me to write this particular book.

THE 4 DEGREES OF RELATIONSHIP

Friends: Choose Godly, Choose Wisely

Contents

Acknowledgement...xxiii

Preface.. xxv

Introduction 1

Chapter 1
How to Handle the Crowds around You 17

Chapter 2
Colleagues, Associates & Comrades... 33

Chapter 3
Your Friends and Companions: Who are they? 45

Chapter 4
Inner Circle of Friends & Confidants 61

Chapter 5
The 5 Dynamics of Friendship (The 5 "C's" Of Friendship) ... 87

Chapter 6
Friends, It is Your Choice, Not Their's. 107

Chapter 7
Moving Beyond Your Past, Stepping into Your Destiny........ 117

ACKNOWLEDGEMENT

Thanks to the following people for your selfless service in making this book a possibility.

Editorial staff:
Andrea Williams (USA), Felicia Amma Antwi (Ghana)

Photography:
Ms. Victoria Nyarko (VFWC)

Cover Design:
Rev. Dean Harvey (ORAC)

To Joan Elaine, my wife, life-long partner and
my greatest counselor.

To my children and greatest admirers, Tori, Joash and Vanya.

To all the precious people of God at
the Victory Family Worship Center.

Your dedication to God and to the sharing of the burden of
the ministry is what gives me the spare time away from some
of my ministerial duties in order to write.

PREFACE

IT'S A MATTER of common knowledge that many of the headaches we go through in life are a result of bad choices we make. This book is about relationships, friendships and associations, which is one of the key areas of our lives that we need to safeguard against the infiltration of the worldly systems and traditions around us. Its key goal is to teach the reader how to model their sphere of relationship after the pattern of Christ.

Some argue that they have only one or two friends, or that they do not have any friends at all, but we all, to some degree, have a sphere of association with other people who have the potential to impact the way we behave and the decisions we make in life.

I totally agree with the popular saying that "no man is an Island," because truly, we are all interconnected in a way that may be beyond our understanding. That is why a normal person will come to the aid of a stranger when they see them stranded in a situation that they could help. That is more so the reason people will put their lives in danger to save others whom they do not even know or have ever met.

One cannot underestimate the importance that Jesus placed on his associates because it is out of his associations that he chose the 12 disciples who he would later refer to as his friends.

It was also out of the 12 disciples that he later chose the 3 disciples (Peter, James and John) who became his inner circle and confidants.

The 6th chapter of the Gospel of Luke made us understand that Jesus took time out to pray all night in order to choose his 12 disciples. Think about that for a moment. If Jesus would pray to God all night for guidance in choosing the men who would be with him for only 3 years of ministry, then doesn't that alone tell us that there is something crucial about relationship and that we ought to pray for God's guidance to choose who should be our friends? If Jesus did not underestimate the subject of relationship but took time to seek God for guidance, then we would be making a big blunder in our lives if we underestimated the impact relationships can make on our lives, or if we see it as being trivial.

Some would argue that friendships develop naturally, but how many of us would like to leave our fate to nature to decide for us while we have the God-given abilities to assess and make wise choices?

Why do we wear light clothing in summer and heavy and warm clothing in the winter? It is because we want to readjust our lives to what nature has to offer in terms of variations in the seasons. The same analogy can be applied to the subject of friendship and our associations with others. It would not be wise nor in our best interest to leave our associations to our natural tendencies to decide for us while we have the God-given ability to alter the impact of nature upon us.

To let the chips fall where they may means to accept defeat without trying.

INTRODUCTION

IN CHOOSING HIS disciples according to Luke 6:12, Jesus prayed all night to God for guidance in order to choose the 12 men he would be with for the space of his 3-year earthly ministry. How many of us cared enough to pray for even a half-night when we were at the point of choosing the spouse with whom we are supposed to spend the rest of our lives? However, one may wonder why, if Jesus prayed all night to choose his disciples, how did he choose the likes of Judas, Thomas, Peter, Matthew and Simon the Zealot?

Thomas was a man full of doubt, and doubt as we know is the direct opposite of faith. So, the question then is, how does a man full of doubt walk together with Jesus who is full of faith?

Simon the Zealot, as his name suggests, was a die-hard political activist who may had joined the Jesus movement most probably to pursue his own political agenda. The Zealots were known to cause riots and political unrest during the Roman rule, in an attempt to overthrow the Roman government. At the time of Jesus, Israel was under Roman governance.

Matthew, as the Bible tells us, was a Tax Collector by profession. In those days tax collectors were branded as society's greatest liars and most corrupt citizens. They were so corrupt that they were despised and hated by the general public, to the extent that a tax collector's testimony was deemed unacceptable in a Jewish court of law. Furthermore, alms given by Tax Collectors and deeds of charity offered by them were deemed unclean.

The **Peter** we know from the pages of Scripture was a man with wavering faith. Although he may have sincerely loved the Lord Jesus, he denied knowing him under oath, which was something almost as serious as Judas' betrayal of Jesus.

On the other hand, the choice of **Judas Iscariot** as one of the 12 disciples is something really mind-boggling if indeed the choices that Jesus made were guided by the hand of God, as Jesus did pray on that subject. That is like Jesus prayed only to choose the devil himself; yet the Bible says Jesus prayed all night for guidance. Judas was a traitor who betrayed his master for 30 pieces of silver.

This is like choosing 12 apples at the market place through careful physical examination, only to get home and find out when they're cut open that about 5 of the 12 apples happened to be below your expectations. That makes us wonder what prayer is all about if one would pray to God for guidance and direction and yet end up with what is least expected.

May the Lord help us to understand prayer and to know that prayer is not about what we *want* but rather about the emergence of God's Kingdom on earth and the fulfillment of His will in our lives. That is why in teaching His disciples to pray, Jesus said to them, "Pray that God's Kingdom come and that His will be done on earth as it is in heaven," Like Jesus, the moment we come to this understanding about prayer, we will be more prepared to embrace the outcome, whether it meets our human expectations or not. The bottom line to prayer is that, the will of God will be accomplished, and so Jesus' prayer in Gethsemane sounded as follows, "If it is possible, let this cup pass away from me, nevertheless, it is not my will but Thine will, Oh Lord, be done."

In brief, that is what prayer means. It is the execution of the will of God on earth and among His people. Anything else outside this expectation is not a proper prayer. Have you ever prayed for the will of God to be done in a situation in which you find yourself and you never cared about what your personal desires might have been? That is a true prayer and it always brings to you the peace of God and His abiding presence when you do so. The next time you pray, try keeping your will out of God's business and see for yourself the peace and harmony that you will feel within your soul.

To delineate the four spheres or degrees of human relationships, and to clearly establish the various groups of people that Jesus had to deal with, let us critically examine Jesus' call of His disciples to ministry as recorded in **Luke 6:12-19.**

*"12] And it came to pass in those days, that he went out into a mountain to pray, and continued all night in prayer to God. [13] And when it was day, he called unto him **His disciples:** and of them **He chose twelve**, whom also He named apostles; [14] Simon, (whom He also named Peter,) and Andrew his brother, James and John, Philip and Bartholomew, [15] Matthew and Thomas, James the son of Alphaeus, and Simeon called Zealots, [16] And Judas the brother of James, and Judas Iscariot, which also was the traitor. [17] And He came down with them, (the 12 Apostles) and stood in the plain, and the company of his disciples, (the 58 left out of the 70) and **a great multitude of people** out of all Judaea and Jerusalem, and from the sea*

coast of Tyre and Sidon, which came to hear him, and to be healed of their diseases, [18] And they that were vexed with unclean spirits: and they were healed. [19] And the whole multitude sought to touch him: for there went virtue out of him, and healed them all.

In the passage of Scripture above, Jesus is about to select **His disciples from His disciples**, which is something I did not notice until a few years ago when I started my studies into the subject of relationship. Prior to that I may have read this passage of Scripture on several occasions and was of the impression that He chose His disciples directly from the crowds of people who were always found following Him wherever he went.

On the contrary and to my utmost surprise, I realized that the 12 disciples were chosen not from the crowd but rather from the 70 disciples that Jesus already had with him. This proves that our knowledge and understanding of God's word comes in dimensions. ***"Precept upon precept, line upon line, here a little, and there a little"*** as proclaimed by the Prophet Isaiah (**Isaiah 28:13**).

This speaks to the reason why we must constantly study the word of God and scratch the surface for deeper and fresher revelation and understanding. Psalm 92:10 puts it this way, ***"But my horn shalt thou exalt like the horn of a unicorn: I shall be anointed with fresh oil."*** Every child of God needs a fresh word and fresh revelation from God every time we dive into the study of His word.

Upon coming down from praying on the mountain, Jesus called to himself all the disciples he had, prior to choosing the 12. Most Bible scholars agree that their number was 70 and out of these 70 disciples, Jesus chose 12. He then went on to name these 12 apostles, comprising Simon (whom he also named Peter,) and Andrew his brother, James and John, Philip and Bartholomew, Matthew and Thomas, James the son of Alphaeus, and Simon called Zealots, Judas the brother of James, and Judas Iscariot, which also was the traitor.

Now notice the demarcation of the various spheres of groups that took place after that, starting from Verse 17 of Luke Chapter 6. Verse 17 reads, **"then he came down to the plains with them** ("them" referred to the 12 that he had just chosen) **from the company of his disciples,** (referring to the ones among the initial 70 disciples that he did not choose.) Meaning they were 58 in number (i.e., 70 minus 12) if indeed Jesus started with 70 disciples, **and the multitudes of people** (the crowds of people that always followed Jesus around).

From there, Jesus' earthly ministry began to take full force and to flow and spread out of Galilee which had served as His base to the rest of Israel. From there, his ministry extended to Judah and to the outermost regions of the Gentile nations of Tyre, Sidon and other places where we are told that He began to heal the sick, and perform all manner of miracles and workings of power. If you notice very carefully you would find out that there are in this passage, 3 degrees of separation among the people Jesus encountered in the passage.

> **"The Apostolic College was formed of three concentric circles, each less closely intimate with Jesus than the last." (Godet)**

In addition to these 3 spheres or degrees of separation of the people, we will come to learn in the Bible and in later chapters of this book that a fourth degree of relational sphere was added by Jesus to the 3 spheres already demarcated in Luke 6, when Jesus later chose Peter, James and John into his inner circle of relationship.

So, in total, one can see here, 4 degrees or spheres of relationship, beginning from the crowds to the 70 disciples, to the 12 who were chosen and finally to the three (Peter, James and John) who eventually became the inner core and confidants of Jesus. *(Refer to Diagram)*

First had they become Friends, then Disciples of the Lord in a wider sense. Afterwards they were called as Apostles to leave all behind (Luke 5:10, 11, 27, 28), but now were united in a distinctly formed circle of Apostles. And even within this there are still grades in respect to their intimate communion with Christ. Even as Apostles, He called them at first Servants (Matt. 10:24), afterwards Friends and Children (John 13:33; 15:15), finally even Brethren (John 20:17). *[Lange Commentary on the Holy Scriptures]*

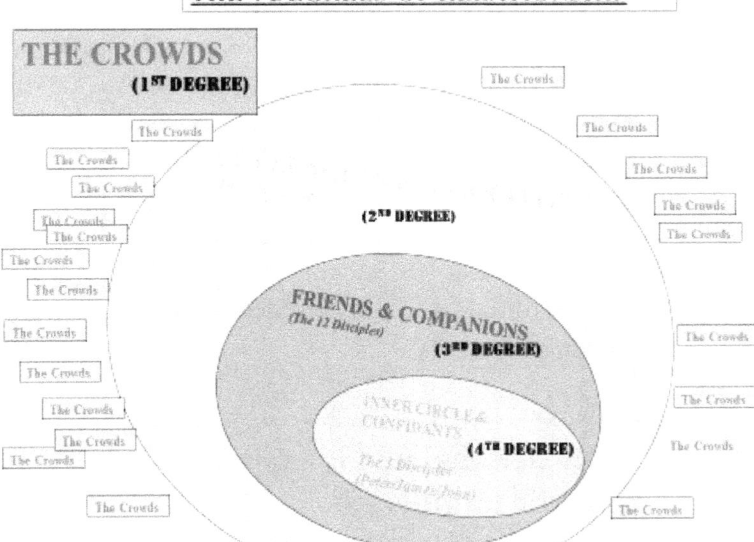

All diagrams are original creation of the Author and may be used or reproduced by permission from the Author.

1st Degree of Relationship: *Crowds & Multitudes*

2nd Degree of Relationship: *Associates & Comrades*

3rd Degree of Relationship: *Friends & Companions*

4th Degree of Relationship: *Inner Circle & Confidants*

In Jesus' sphere of relationship, the Crowds are represented by the multitudes that followed Jesus. The Associates are represented by the 58 disciples who were part of the original 70 but who were not chosen among the 12. The Friends and

Companions are represented by the 12 disciples who later became the 12 Apostles of the Lamb. Finally, the Inner Circle and Confidants were represented by the 3 disciples (Peter, James and John) who were closest to Jesus and who Jesus always called along to accompany him during very critical and important occasions.

So, Jesus first chose the 70 from the crowd, then went beyond the 70 and out of them, chose 12. The 12 disciples are closer to him than the 70 but later we will come to find that some were not the closest to him. Here, Jesus teaches us a beautiful lesson about relationships.

The Closer the relationship gets, the lesser the number.

Notice that the number goes down drastically from a crowd of people to 70 disciples, then to 12 disciples. I delved a little further and showed you that even from the 12 disciples closest to him, Jesus further selected 3, Peter, James and John, and brought them much closer to himself as possible.

The closer the relationship gets, the more the energy and virtue it takes out of you; that explains why you cannot bring a cluster of people into your inner circle. If you do, they will drain all your energy, time and resources although they have no level of commitment to you. If Jesus had the capacity to handle only 3 disciples in his inner circle, then you ought to think very carefully about the host of people you have in your inner circle.

This relationship model of Jesus is very practical because there were obviously some things that Jesus wanted the three men in the inner core of Disciples to know and see, but not the 12, nor the 70, nor the crowds. It's a matter of common knowledge that not everything can be open and shared with everybody.

This also means that you cannot share your dreams and aspirations with just anyone. You may have to live with the consequences if you do. If you do not agree with me on this statement, just look into the life of the popular Bible character by the name of Joseph and see what happened to him as a result of openly sharing his dreams with his own brothers.

How do you know what to share, or not to share, and who to share with or who not to share with? I will expound on the answers to these questions in a later chapter, but the baseline is that you should keep your eyes open and watch the kind of signals that come from the people you meet and let the Lord lead and guide you in your choice of friends and associations.

As an example, there are "friends" who respond to any text message or email you send them about any mishap in your life or ministry. But they don't respond to messages that have to do with some great accomplishment or testimony of something the Lord has done or is doing in your life or ministry. When it is something good and positive, they do not see the need to join in on the conversation, but God forbid—if it is something bad or negative, they will be quick to respond and join in the conversation. This is because that's what makes them feel like they are getting ahead of you.

The book of **Proverbs 14:33** declares that ***"Wisdom resteth in the heart of him that hath understanding."*** If this is true for us, then the earlier you rise up to the subject of friendship, the better and easier your life will be.

....

If you really want to reach your God-given potential and fully realize your destiny in life; then that will mean you cannot walk along with just any and everyone.

....

The reasons for the above statement is:

1. **You cannot be a David until you find a Jonathan.**

   We all need the right associations to help elevate us to the level where God wants us to be. This is simply because *you were raised outside the Palace; and you may need a Jonathan to set you over the walls into the Palace—which is the place of your destiny. Even when you get into the Palace, you may still need a Jonathan to protect you from the wicked spear and javelin of a King who is intoxicated with wickedness like King Saul. Except for the fact that David was protected from the devices of King Saul, he would have perished in the Palace.*

2. **We all need a Jonathan in order to avoid many of the headaches we go through in life, which comes from wrong associations.**

   The kind of people we hang around with and share association with make all the difference.

Many people have surrounded themselves with people who should not be around them. Even in the Church, you have to be careful who your associations are because not all Israel is indeed Israel. This is in a way a hard thing to say about associations in the Church. But just like the exodus of the children of Israel from Egypt represented the Church and yet there were mixed multitudes among them who did not trust or worship the God of Israel, so it is in the Church today. Here is the fundamental principle or the baseline when it comes to relationships; it is found in **Galatians 6:10:** ***"As we have therefore opportunity, let us do good unto all men . . . "***

This is the baseline, because as Christians, it is expected that we respect all people, acknowledge all people and treat all people well, with respect and with dignity. This is the common baseline that we ought to abide by. More often than not, we find out that we have faulty relationships because the subject of relationship and friendship has been either greatly misunderstood or wrongly defined by many. Good and positive relationships are those that are based on understanding rather than emotions. That's why there is so much drama and so many relationship headaches in our world or circles of relationships these days.

Sometimes we are made to believe that relationships are driven by *emotions*. So, people come around you and show a whole lot of emotions and that makes you feel good and consider them friends. But the key to a wise and healthy relationship is not *Emotion*. It is *understanding*. Therefore, relationships ought to be driven by *understanding*, not *emotion*. Look at what the Bible says about that: *"Can two walk together, except they be agreed?" Amos 3:3.*

When there is no mutual understanding or agreement in terms of boundaries, unfulfilled expectations are inevitable

What we have become is a generation of spiritual fanatics who blame the devil for every mistake we make in life, while at the same time, rejecting the knowledge we need, and that is accessible to us in order to do well. I hate to sound like I am playing the devil's advocate, but we cannot ignore the opportunities and resources that are available to make us better people and simply blame every predicament on the devil. This is because not every storm that comes to us, or that we go through comes from the devil. While there is no argument that some storms may be of demonic origins because they are engineered and propelled by the devil, other storms may be developmental while still others may be decisional storms.

Decisional storms are storms that arrive as a result of bad decisions or even good decisions, since good decisions can also bring storms into our lives through the challenges that at times come along with them. Developmental storms on the other hand, are storms that God himself puts the believer through so He can build character.

"But the God of all grace, who hath called us unto His eternal glory by Christ Jesus, after that ye have suffered a while, make you perfect, stablish, strengthen, settle you," (**1 Peter 5:10**)

An example of a developmental storm is what Joseph went through both at the hands of his brothers and in Potiphar's house at the hands of Mrs. Potiphar.

There are times when God does take us through this particular kind of storm simply to prove to us that "ye are not bastards but rather sons and daughters of his Kingdom." Consider this Scripture, *"But if ye be without chastisement, whereof all are partakers, then are ye bastards, and not sons."* (**Hebrews 12:8**)

Also, surprisingly at times, God takes us through storms just so he can boast about us to Satan. Remember what happened to Job? That is the type of storm that he went through. In other words, God and Satan were having their own dialogue and Job's name just happened to come up by accident. ***"Hast thou considered my servant Job?"*** and then you know the story. It is Job who ended up suffering because of the conversation between God and Satan. He went through all these sufferings simply because God decided to boast about him to devil.

Have you ever wondered how life would be for you should God decide to boast about you to Satan? Would you break apart, hate everyone around you, curse God and die like Job's wife suggested to Job? Or would you hold up to your faith and integrity in God?

So therefore, the implication here is that success and failure in life leans heavily upon our associations, the kind of people we associate ourselves with. Look at it this way, **"He that walketh with wise men shall be wise: but a companion of fools shall be destroyed." (Proverbs 13:20).** The Bible did not say, "the companion of fools will be foolish," It says they shall be destroyed, because it is pointing to the ultimate end of those who choose their companions unwisely.

Jesus told the disciple that he called them to become fishers of men, and that would mean every man would have to have a network of people around them in order to become fishers of men. However, there is a caveat here, and that is, your network in life is what is going to determine whether your net will work or not work. Meaning, the people you network with will have a strong role to play in whether you are going to be successful in what you do or fail.

So, what you must do in order to succeed is to carefully examine the type of people you have in your sphere of relationship in order to trim or drop some of them if need be.

This may sound harsh to you when you hear it for the first time, but it will bless your soul and save you from many troubles that lie ahead if you should continue on the path of unwise and unhealthy relationships. Always remember that the people you have around you, will either strengthen you or destroy you. They will either uphold your net or break your net.

Have you ever thought of the fact that God has specially assigned certain people to your life? That means you can't pick up just anybody along the way to be your friend or companion. This assignment is important because the person(s) that God assigns to your life, have the *capacity* to be with you. That means that all others around you who should not be around you are only wasting your time, energy and resources.

At times there are people around us who just do not have the capacity to understand us. However, they hang around because we have allowed it to be so. Watch those people because they are the very people who are going to kill your dreams and aspirations. They are dream killers. Why? Because at times it is just a feel-good thing for you to have so many people around you while what the Lord is trying to say to you is, *"You need to trim down your friendship circles so that you can grow and bear fruit."* Notice that unless the branches of a tree are trimmed down, they really do not experience healthy growth. Therefore, what you need to do is to enter into your friendship closet and trim down some of the people around you in order to advance and achieve your God-given purpose in life.

At times people feel this morbid obligation towards other people and that causes them to cave in to relationships that they know are not going to work out well. However, this is nothing more than just being morbid, unwholesome, and gruesome. At times people feel if they do not give in and yield to the advances of others towards them, they will be labelled as intolerant or unfriendly, so they just do it for the sake of saving face. To save your face and not save your life is definitely not wise, so stand for the good virtues that you believe in.

Good Friendship is not supposed to be a buddy-buddy system. The rise of social media has made it to appear so, but relationships are supposed to be covenantal. Jonathan gave David his own coat or royal robe to wear in order to protect him from the anger of his father, King Saul. The Bible says that on that day David made a covenant with Jonathan. The sad thing is that people are tearing you down and destroying you and yet you still keep going back to them.

Comparing the 4 spheres of relationships it is worth noting that the bond formed with the crowds in one's sphere of relationship is very weak. This is because, unlike the spheres representing the second, third, and fourth degrees of relationship, the sphere representing the crowds has an inner boundary that it shares with the second sphere (i.e. Associates/Colleagues) but it has no outer boundary. This means that it is totally open to the elements on the outside world.

The spheres representing the second and third degrees of relationships, which are your colleagues and friends respectively, both have outer and inner boundaries. The implication here is that the bonds formed within these spheres of relationships are stronger than the bond formed with the crowds.

Finally, notice that the fourth sphere of relationship, represented by one's inner circle of friends and confidants, is different from the other spheres of relationship, represented by one's colleagues and friends in that it has only one boundary (an outer boundary). Although it has one boundary like the sphere represented by the crowds, it is a far stronger bond than the bond that exists between all the other spheres of relationship. Despite the fact that it has only one boundary as found in the first degree of relationship (Crowds), it is different from the crowds in that the boundary is an outer boundary instead of an inner boundary as in the first degree of relationship.

What this means is that the one outer boundary protects all the content of information and knowledge imbedded within this sphere of relationship. The outer boundary protects the privacy and confidentiality of the relationship between a person and his or her inner circle of friends and confidants. It also has no other boundary besides the outer boundary because relationships at this level are meant to be for the long haul. Hence, once you enter into this sphere of relationship, an escape through any other exit is possible, but not expected.

CHAPTER 1

HOW TO HANDLE THE CROWDS AROUND YOU

Our Text: **Luke 6:12-19**

*[17] And He (Jesus) came down with them, (the 12 Apostles) and stood in the plain, and the company of His disciples, (the 58 left out of the 70) and **a great multitude of people** out of all Judaea and Jerusalem, and from the sea coast of Tyre and Sidon, which came to hear him, and to be healed of their diseases.*

THE FIRST DEGREE of relationship that exists in the human circle of relationships are the crowds. They are also referred to as the multitude, the masses, and every one of us have them around us in one way or the other. So, who are they? These are all the people we know casually, all the people we come across and have some level of encounter with on daily basis. Jesus said about the crowd, when it comes to relationships, they connect with you simply because they have a need in their lives that needs to be met. Notice, I did not say they like you or wish you well. They simply have a need and they will go anywhere, follow any agenda, and attach themselves to anyone if they foresee chances of having their needs met through the association.

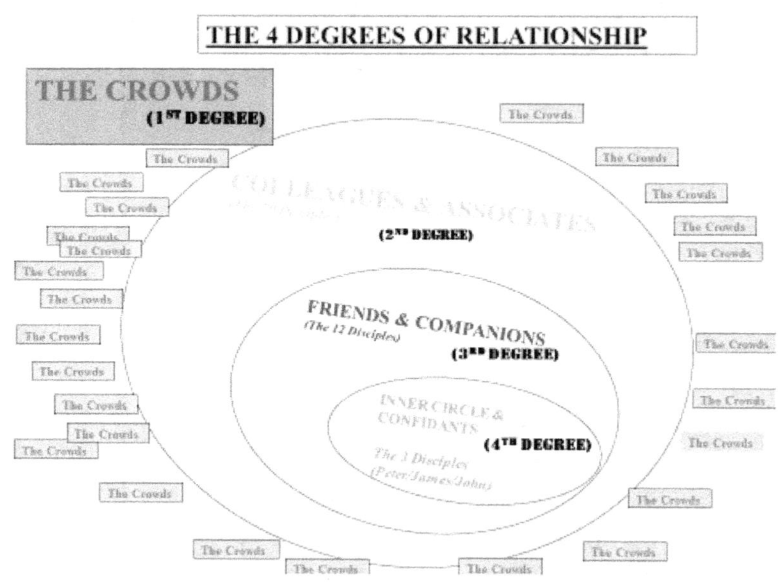

All diagrams are original creation of the Author and may be used or reproduced by permission from the Author.

It is never strange at all to find people connecting with other people that they do not like. This is so, simply because they have a need in their lives.

These are the people that Jesus calls "the fish and bread crowd." The day after Jesus performed the miracle of multiplying the fish and the loaves of bread for the multitude to eat, the people followed after Jesus and when they did not find him at the spot where he had performed the miracle, they took a boat and followed after him across the waters to the other side where they heard he was. When they finally found Him, they said to Jesus, we have been looking for you all day and we are glad we found You. Jesus, knowing their motive, said to them, ***"Jesus answered them and said, Verily, verily, I say unto you, Ye seek me, not because ye saw the miracles, but because ye did eat of the loaves, and were filled." (John 6:26)***

That is when he cautioned them with a stern rebuke by saying to them, ***"Labour not for the meat which perisheth, but for that meat which endureth unto everlasting life, which the Son of man shall give unto you: for him hath God the Father sealed. (John 6:27)***

What Jesus was demonstrating here was that the fish and bread crowds, after their needs have been met, might leave you. This therefore leads me to say the following:

When people walk away from you, do not fall apart; their departure should be an opportunity for you to assess whether they were truly with you in the first place.

Their departure should help you to assess what group or sphere of relationship they belong to when they were around you. It should lead you to ask questions like, were they really your friends, were they just your associates, or were they in the crowds around you? Assessing my own experience with people,

I think I have experienced so much of these in my life as well as in my ministry and that gives me the audacity to write on this subject.

Watch what happens next, when the crowds realized that they are not going to get any more free bread and fish from Jesus after they had spent all day chasing after Him. This story is very interesting in that it totally reveals the prime motive of the crowds of people one has in their relationship circles.

> **66. From that time, many of his disciples went back, and walked no more with him. 67. Then said Jesus unto the twelve, will ye also go away? 68. Then Simon Peter answered him, Lord, to whom." (John 6: 66-68)**

Verse 66 declares that from that time onwards many of his disciples went back and walked no more with Jesus. And that was what propelled Jesus to assess his relationship with the remaining disciples in order to make sure that those left with him were really with him and not following him for their personal gains. For Jesus, people walking away from him was an opportunity to do a critical assessment by questioning the motive of those remaining when he asked them, *67] Then said Jesus unto the twelve, Will ye also go away?*

This is why I mentioned earlier in this chapter that when people walk away from you, do not fall apart because it is an opportunity to do a personal relationship assessment. If they brazenly walked away from Jesus, then do not be taken by surprise or shock when they walk away from you. That is actually just the nature of the crowd, because one of the key characteristics of the crowd is that they are supposed to be fickle. Being fickle means they are causally and erratically changeable. They are not stable, nor are they loyal in their affection.

At times, people wonder why it is that after they have invested into the lives of others, they have no one to give back to them. It's because you may have sown and invested your time, energy and resources into the crowds and the crowds by their nature are not looking to give back. They are around you only for their own benefit and after that benefit is drawn, they are gone.

Watch the crowds in your sphere of relationship because they have the tendency to change on you at the drop of a dime. One day, they'll seem to be all over you and all for you and on another day, they are nowhere to be found. They will be all around you when you are in your season of winning, but when you hit rock bottom in your season of loss, they will be gone before you look around. If this description rings a bell in your mind about anybody you know, then be sure that they belong to the crowd.

Quit worrying about the people who leave you or the people God intentionally took away from you and be thankful for the people God sends your way.

If indeed the paths that you tread are ordained by God, then we ought to follow the lead and directions of God in choosing our friends and associates.

Not every door God opens in front of you is meant for you to walk through and not every opportunity is a blessing.

As an illustration, one must realize that not all doors that God opens to us are meant for us to walk through. This statement seems like it makes no sense logically because if God opened a door before us, then why would He not intend for us to walk through? One may even ask, what good is an open door to me if it is not intended for me to walk through?

This is why, at times, God may open a door before you, but it is not for you to walk through. It may be intended for those people who are hanging around you but are not ordained by God to be with you, to go through that open door. Usually, the moment they go through that door, God shuts the door behind them, so He will be able to lead you into your destiny without them. I hope it now makes sense to you why a door may be opened before you but at the same time, is not intended for you to walk through. The reverse may also be true, in that God may close a door behind you simply to keep away from you the very elements that are hindering you from fulfilling His purpose in your life. That in a sense is so beautiful because, although it is a closed door, it is not a closed or lost opportunity. It is only a closed door leading to an opened opportunity.

You will generally find the crowds around you when you have a lot and things are going well with you. But when you are in your season of loss, they may be quick to tell you how the Lord spoke to them in some sort of manner and asked them to move on away from you. Therefore, in your dealings with the crowd, be very careful not to assign the word "friend" to the crowds. Otherwise you are going to be greatly disappointed. It is not even necessary to assign the word "friend" to your "colleagues," even though they are a bit closer to you than the crowd.

Biblical Examples of the Crowd:

1. Orpah.

As a way of introduction to this Bible personage, Orpah was one of the two daughters-in-law of Naomi. The other was Ruth. Because of the number of tragedies that Naomi went through, which stemmed from the death of her husband, and then followed by the sudden deaths of her two sons, she decided to refrain from the land of Moab to Bethlehem where she and her family had originally journeyed from. Both Naomi's daughters-in-law, Orpah and Ruth, decided to follow her back to her native city of Bethlehem but Naomi tried to convince them to both stay back and carry on with their lives.

However, what convinced Orpah to return from following her mother-in-law was the moment Orpah was told by Naomi that, "I am too old to produce another son for you to be married to and even if I did, you could not wait till he become a man." In other words, Naomi was trying to convince Orpah that she would draw no benefit from following her since there was nothing to gain in following her. That was enough to get Orpah to go packing her stuff to leave her mother-in-law, Naomi. On the other hand, the fact that Naomi was old and was never going to bear any more sons for the daughters-in-law to be married to, meant nothing to a true companion and friend like Ruth.

What got Orpah to go packing her bag to abandon her mother-in-law was the same that propelled Ruth to cleave unto her mother-in-law. Think a moment about the actions of these two daughters-in-law. According to Ruth 1:14, while Orpah kissed her mother-in-law and bid her farewell on her journey back to Bethlehem, Ruth on the other hand clave unto her.

That was what inspired Ruth to utter those immortal words as recorded in **Ruth 1:14-17 (KJV)**

> *16) "Entreat me not to leave thee, or to return from following after thee: for whither thou goest, I will go, and where thou lodgest, I will lodge: thy people shall be my people, and thy God my God: [17] Where thou diest, will I die, and there will I be buried: the Lord do so to me, and more also, if ought but death part thee and me. where thou lodgest, will I lodge"*

From this beautiful story, one can see clearly the motives of the crowds when they are following you. Since Orpah belonged to the crowds, it was very easy to get her to refrain from following her mother-in-law when she found out that there might not be any personal benefit for her in following Naomi. Ruth, on the other hand, saw it as an opportunity to show Naomi how much she loved and cared for her through those immortal words which have become one of Scripture's most quoted verses of the Bible. It is ironic that what sent one leaving is the same that made the other cleave.

2. During Jesus' Triumphant Entry into Jerusalem:

When you read the gospel accounts of Jesus' triumphant entry into Jerusalem (Bible Text) you will find that it was the crowd around Jesus that chanted "Hosanna, hosanna in the Highest blessed is he that cometh in the name of the Lord," because the Jews were under Roman rule and governance at the time and they had a need for a King who would deliver them from the hands of their oppressors.

A matter of seven (7) days later, they realized that their

wishes of crowning Jesus as the King of the Jews was not going to materialize. Instead, they chanted, "crucify him, crucify him." The question that one may ask is that, "What did they miss in 7 days?" The crowd that chanted "Hosanna, hosanna in the Highest—blessed is he that cometh in the name of the Lord," just a few days earlier was now chanting for Jesus of Nazareth to be crucified. What went wrong within a matter of few days? It was simply because what they thought would be a gain for them and all their hopes of having a political deliverer in the person of Jesus of Nazareth, had been eroded, to be replaced by the doom of His impending crucifixion that lay ahead on the rugged cross on the hills of Calvary.

That's just the nature of crowds. They are fickle in every sense of the word. They're not meant to be with you; neither are they interested in you. They are only around because they have a need that needs to be met and once that need is met, or they see signs that their needs are not going to be met through you, they will leave you. Again, be sure not to fall apart, because in most cases, their departure is *their* loss, not your loss, since they were not meant to be with you in the first place.

O' how I wish this saying would register louder in your spirit, because many people go through the feeling of helplessness and hopelessness when others in their sphere of relationships for one reason or the other walk away. Remember that, like Jesus, those times in your life should be moments of self-assessment instead of self-pity. Quit pitying yourself because people decided to walk away from you, and begin to assess yourself in order to strengthen your relationship with those who are meant to be with you.

How to Connect with the Crowds

The fact that everyone of us has crowds around us and that there is always going to be a crowd within our sphere of relationship is inevitable. As such, I wouldn't want to close this chapter without first showing you how to connect with the crowds and how to handle the crowds around you. This is how you connect to the crowds—when it comes to your relationship with the crowds, you connect to the crowds indirectly. If not, they will drain every iota of energy, time and resources out of you and leave you empty and destitute.

In fact, when you look at the 12 disciples that Jesus chose to be with him, one of the first assignments that Jesus gave them was to handle the crowds and multitudes of people that followed Him. That's why you would notice in the Bible that occasionally they would try to turn people away from the Lord. On the occasion when they tried to turn the children away from Jesus, He quickly intervened and said, ***"Forbid not the little children to come to me for of such is the Kingdom of Heaven"*** **(Matthew 19:14).**

On another occasion, they tried to stop the Syrophoenician woman from seeing Jesus because they thought He needed some rest, and again Jesus had to intervene by meeting the woman's need. The only time Jesus dealt directly with the crowds was when the disciples failed to deal with them adequately. That's why Jesus had to step in and deal with the Syrophoenician woman directly.

Lessons to be learnt.

....

You cannot bring the crowds into your intimate sphere of relationship because, with every relationship comes a measure of withdrawal and impartation.

....

Facebook, Twitter and in fact, social media in general has gotten us going *crazy* because it is teaching us the impossibility of having thousands, ten thousands and hundreds of thousands of people in our sphere of relationship, although that's electronically and technologically possible in a way, it is not humanly beneficial because with every human relationship and encounter there comes a withdrawal of virtue out of you.

When Jesus had to deal with mobs of people who followed Him, He would say things like, virtue is gone out of him: remember? If that is true for Jesus, it means it is also true in your case. You cannot be spending your time, energy and virtue in dealing with hundreds and thousands of people via social media and still have enough time and energy available to tackle the important things in life. Although I am not on any of the major social media sites such as Facebook or Twitter, at times, the volume of text messages that come to me through regular texts and the "Whats App" alone are enough to either distract me or put me in a stressful condition and mood simply because every relationship requires a measure of withdrawal and impartation.

If I am to literally use the pattern of Jesus' sphere of relationship as a model, then I would say, you don't have the capacity to go beyond 12 people in your circle of friendship and 3 people in your inner circles of friendship. What technology and all these social media networking sites do is they create an abstract and superficial world around us. This is what I call a "balloon or bubble relationship." It looks big and humongous as though you are in touch with the whole world, and yet it lacks reality and tangibility. That's why these days you would often hear people boasting about the thousands and tens of thousands and hundreds of thousands of friends and followers that they have through social media. However, the question they ought to ask themselves is, how many of these people that they are boasting about have they ever met? Also, how many of the so-called followers, if any, would be around for them when they are going through their low seasons, moments of loss or disappointments in life?

The Scripture says in Matthew Chapter 24:12, ***"And because iniquity shall abound, the love of many shall wax cold."*** This does not necessarily mean sin shall be so plentiful to the extent that people are going to be walking around naked in public. This means that what is going to be one of the notable characteristics of the end time is that people are going to have superficial or balloon relationships and thereby make it easy for them not to be able to connect with the real people around them. That's why it's becoming so prevalent to see people seriously engaged with chatting with people on social media whom they don't know and have never met, while ignoring others who are right next to them. Already, many young people are caught up in this "balloon and superficial" world to the extent that they are ignoring real life friends, dear ones who care for them, families, siblings, and others who are immediately around them.

Have you ever thought, and has it ever dawned on you that the follower on Facebook and Twitter that you have been *wasting* a big chunk of your time and energy to chat with on regular basis could be a rapist, pedophile, murderer or someone with a very dangerous and wicked personality? The goal of this chapter is to get you thinking about some of these dangers and possibilities in the superficial world of social media.

I am thankful to God for this revelation on relationships because I can't afford to be fooled by the crowds that are in my sphere of relationship. I know who my friends are, from the crowds that are around me. In addition, I hold in high esteem the faithful brethren, friends and associates in ministry that I have gotten to know over the years, as well as the genuine new ones that I am getting to meet and to know from day to day. Hence, I will not be fooled by the motives of the fake ones who pass through the Church and who I meet at various places from time to time.

I must say that there is nothing wrong with people passing through a church to assess if it is the right congregation for them. However, at times they make you feel comfortable with their presence, as if to say they are with you and into your vision. Then, in the next moment, they will drop you like a piece of cake and leave you for their own selfish agendas.

After all the experiences that I have been through over the years, I know those who are with me when I see them. Not only do I see them around with my eyes, but it's as if I can also feel their presence and support even when for some unforeseen reasons, they happened not to be physically present with me. These faithful people are my trophies in ministry and my precious Jewels of ministry. They are those that I can call my friends and true companions.

In conclusion, what I suggest you do in order to make headway into your God-given destiny and to be able to move on to the next spiritual level, is to assess your relationship circles and to drop some friends who are not on the same wavelength with you as far as your ambition for God is concerned. It is my prayer that the Lord will direct us to men and women that He has ordained to be with us and who have the capacity to walk with us. May the Lord help us to clear up our relationship closet and rejuvenate our circle of friendship and associations so He can lead us to His chosen and anointed men and women who will drive us into bearing godly fruits unto salvation.

'Food-For-Thought'
Worksheet for Chapter 1

1. Can you identify the people around you who fall within your first circle of relationship? (The "Crowds")

2. Make a list of these people.

3. On what level do you relate with these people, directly or indirectly?

4. Are they influencing your life in any positive way?

5. List four ways, if any, by which they are positively influencing your life.

6. If you cannot come up with at least two ways through which your association with them has positively influenced your life, then chances are, either they are wasting your time and energy, or you are wasting theirs.

7. Be mindful about the crowd of people in your life. They are time and energy deflectors.

8. List a couple of people that you have come across in your life who fall within the first circle of friendship.

i) ________________   v) ________________

ii) ________________   vi) ________________

iii) ________________   vii) ________________

iv) ________________   viii) ________________

Note: A maximum of eight names are required to be entered because, according to the role of friendship, one would expect encounter with more people within the first sphere of relationship.

(Refer to diagram at the beginning of this chapter and the various characteristics of the people who fall within the first sphere of relationship mentioned throughout the first chapter of this book)

CHAPTER 2
COLLEAGUES, ASSOCIATES & COMRADES

YOUR COMRADES FORM the second degree in your sphere of human relationships. Another word for this sphere of people you relate with is the word "Associates." They are represented by the 58 Disciples that Jesus did not choose to be part of the 12 Apostles of the Lamb.

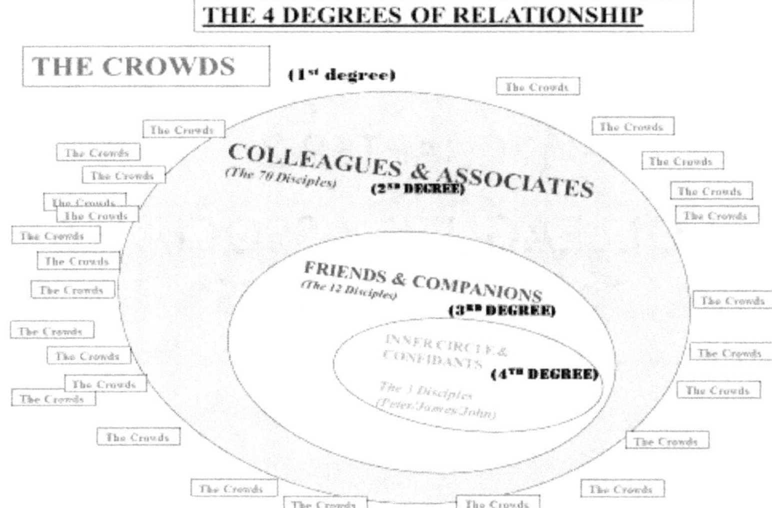

All diagrams are original creation of the author and may be used or reproduced by permission from the author.

These are the people you work with. They are also the members of staff, or of a team whether it is academia, work, sports or otherwise.

At work: they are your colleagues or co-workers.

At school: they are your classmates, course mates or schoolmates.

In business: they are your associates or business partners.

In sports: they are your teammates.

In other areas: they are simply your comrades.

The etymology of the word associate originates from the French word "colleague" meaning, "being of the same school of thought." Therefore, you and your colleagues or associates are brought together by a common goal to accomplish a defined task. The problem begins however, when one attempts to take this relationship beyond what it's supposed to be. For instance, when co-workers begin to turn their work relationship into romance, it more often than not ends up in a relational shipwreck simply because the workplace is not the right setting for romance.

Some time ago, I came across research on romantic relationships in the workplace and this research indicated that the average workplace romances last for 53 days. Although the validity of this conclusion is debatable, it is a matter of common knowledge that most workplace romances don't last nor end well. When you and your co-workers meet on the job, the goal is supposed to be work and work only, because that's the reason why you are brought together in the first place.

That's why most Psychologists will tell you that when you meet someone on the job who you realize you want to get involved with in a romantic kind of relationship, the best thing to do to keep that romantic flame alive is for one of you to find another job and move away from working together. Be careful when dealing with your colleagues. Because you work with them does not mean you should be intimate with them.

Even the people in the workplace knows that it's not a good idea to get intimate or romantically involved with your colleagues. This is especially true when the relationship is between a co-worker and their supervisor or vice versa. That's why this kind of relationship is strongly discouraged by many employers. The Corporations, Industries, Employers of the general workforce know that going out with your subordinate or supervisor is not a good idea, because it affects your ability to make sound work-related decisions and judgement about the person you may be involved with. No employer would want to be paying you at the end of every week for playing romance on the job instead of working.

At times, people use terms like "we are family" on the job, but honestly the people on the job are not family no matter how well they seem to relate to you. The next time a co-worker says that to you on the job, just tell them politely that, "Yes, we both know we are not family." You may sound as if you are being rude, but that's the truth and they know it is the truth. This truth will save you a whole lot of problems and headaches in the future and it may even save you your job down the line if you stick to this truth.

It means then that these sets of people called colleagues or associates are in your life because of work, business, school, or some sort of non-personal association. As a word of caution, don't be surprised if you happen to meet such people even in the Church too. You may be wondering, how is that possible? These are people who may have joined the church not because of their desire to serve the Lord and to know Him better but rather for some self-motivated interest which others already in the church may also happen to share.

Perhaps they are in church just to find a wife or husband. This is not a bad thing, except that it shouldn't be the motivating factor for being in Church. Probably they are in church just as a hang-out because they are lonely. This is also not bad except that it shouldn't be their prime and motivating factor. These are those who would leave you for the slightest thing that happens.

Some time ago, a fellow who had been worshipping with us for a couple of years decided to leave our Church all of a sudden. Over the years that this fellow had been with our Church as a Church officer, I allowed him to sit at the front where I and other ministers would usually sit. However, I realized that for whatever reason, he would usually rush out of service while I was at the podium still preaching, and would walk right past the front into the middle row and then go down the aisle. After repeated occurrences I noticed that this was causing a big distraction to many since he would usually walk directly past the podium and all the way down the aisle in the middle of my sermons. I therefore called him aside and spoke to him politely about this behavior and how it was becoming a distraction to many. I therefore took that opportunity to advise him that he could still sit at the front row where the ministers sat; however, if he knew that he would be leaving service before the sermon ended on Sundays, he may want to move to the back seat at the time I was invited to the podium to preach. Then his walking out of service while the sermon was still in progress would not distract anyone.

He took my advice and did that for a few weeks. Then he stopped coming to Church for a while. He next requested what he claimed to be an urgent meeting with me. When I enquired from him about his reason for his decision to leave, I was totally taken by surprise at what his response was and how trivial a reason for one to want to leave a Church, if indeed they were truly there for the right reasons. He told me that he was leaving our Church because I had asked him to sit in the back row whenever I was about to preach so his departure from service in the middle of my sermon wouldn't distract others. I asked him if he was sure that this was the reason why he was leaving.

If you allow yourself to be taken by devastation because people leave you, you will not make progress. That is why I keep repeating the statement in this book, which is "when people walk away from you, be careful not to fall apart." Rather, on a positive note, see it as an opportunity to assess your sphere of relationship. I have come to realize that for many who leave, it is usually their loss and not mine because they were usually at the receiving end, gaining far more benefit from their association with me than I did from their presence. How did I know that some who left were benefiting from their association with me more than I was? Because from time to time, some of them returned and when they came around this time, they were more sober and thankful for the regained association.

Your colleagues or associates are therefore close to you because of work or some common function that you ought to do together. Since work is multi-faceted, it means this function can be anything ranging from business, industry, private practice or even the work of the ministry of the Church or anything that you have a function to play and they likewise have a function to play in it. It is worth noting that your colleagues, associates or comrades are closer to you than the crowds, but they are not as close to you as your friends and companions. Therefore, if you mistake them for your friends, you will be grossly disappointed.

> **What you must understand is that while you connect with the crowds indirectly, your connection with your colleagues and associates is functional.**

Always have it at the back of your mind that the reason why they are in your life is because there is a function for you to do, and there is a function for them to do and together your functionality produces an expected outcome. Also note that while the crowds around you are supposed to be fickle, your colleagues are not fickle like the crowds. They are more functional. If you want to get the work done, they are there to help get it done by playing their role or performing their function.

Always remember that they are your colleagues because you both belong to the same school of thought and share the same ideology. If you ever try to bring them beyond that sphere of relationship, you would be begging for trouble on the job or on whatever project or causes you are both working on.

The Two Sides of Comradeship

1. The First side.

Usually, your comrades, colleagues or associates are for what you are for, and as long as you are for what they are for, they will team up with you, walk with you and work with you to achieve that common goal. However, there is a caveat here and that is, because they are not for you, but simply for what you are for, when they meet someone else who they feel has the capacity to help advance their agenda or interest to the next higher level, chances are, they'll leave you to join up with the other fellow.

You and your comrades are brought together by a common interest and that bond is relationally weak because it is based on your functions rather than your love and care for one another.

This plays out very often in associations that are business related and profit driven. Their admiration for you or their liking you would not be enough to hold them back from leaving. They would drop you like a hot cake because their association with you is not about you as a person but rather about that common goal and interest that you both happened to share.

This bond is weak because people's interests change from time to time. Today, they may be interested in one thing and months or years later, they may have no interest at all in that same thing. Therefore, don't be shocked when they leave you and move on because they never had your personal well-being at heart, nor were they for you in the first place.

2. The flip side

The flip side of the relationship described above is when your colleagues or associates are not for you nor for what you are for. However, they are associated with you only because they are against what you are against. This kind of relationship with your colleagues and associates is very tricky because although they are not for you nor what you are for, they are connected to you and you to them because there is still a common interest. They're in opposition to what you are in opposition to, and that's enough to establish a common ground for collaboration to accomplish a function, task or goal. They will team up with you to help fight a greater enemy or for a greater cause but again, don't mistake them for friends or companions because they don't care about you. They only care about the cause that you both are in opposition to.

So goes the popular saying that, "*The enemy of your enemy is not necessarily your friend.*" Be careful when dealing with your colleagues and associates under these conditions or circumstances. The only common grounds here are that you both happen to dislike the same thing, person or cause. Hence, they will only be with you until the victory is won and then they will disappear suddenly. The bond between this relationship, like the other before, is also weak in that it's still not about you but rather about a common goal or interest.

I once heard someone compare the role of people in our lives who fall under this sphere of relationship to a scaffold erected on the surface of a building during renovation or construction. In other words, your colleagues and associates come into your life to fulfill a purpose, and like the scaffold, when the renovation or construction is done, they are detached and removed from the building. But even under that condition, don't be upset, discouraged, or disappointed when they are removed from you because the building always remains even after the scaffold is gone. Therefore, let this fact be a consolation to you after your colleagues and associates leave you.

Lastly, when you are dealing with these associates, colleagues or comrades of yours, be careful not to share your dreams, visions and aspirations with them. Because before you know it, they may either discourage you out of it or steal your dreams, visions, and ideas and run with them. Many are those who have blamed themselves and live with regrets for sharing their ideas and innovations with people that they thought had their interest at hand. Don't be a victim to the onslaught of unwise and unhealthy relationships.

'Food-For-Thought'

Worksheet for Chapter 2

1. With guidance from this chapter, list the most common areas of your life where you may encounter people who fall within the second circle of relationship known as your colleagues, associates or comrades.

2. Is your association with this circle of people based solely on your functions, roles, responsibilities or on a personal level?

3. List at least four kinds of subjects you usually discuss with your colleagues or associates.

    i.   _______________________________________

    ii.   _______________________________________

    iii. _______________________________________

    iv.   _______________________________________

4. Are they personal and intimate or are they related to your functions and their functions, role or responsibilities?

5. If your relationship with your colleagues, associates or comrades becomes personal and intimate, it is a sign of your vulnerability to problems associated with taking the relationship beyond what it is supposed to be for that circle of relationship.

6. What then are you supposed to do when the relationship with your colleagues becomes intimate:

   i.   Keep it functional

   ii. Let work remain as work and nothing else

   iii. Refrain from conversations that are personal and intimate

   iv. Always remind yourself that you are there to play a function and focus on the excellent execution of that function.

7. List a few people that you are associated with who fall within the second sphere of friendship.

   (Refer to shaded portion of diagram at the beginning of this chapter and the various characteristics of Colleagues, Associates, and Comrades mentioned throughout the second chapter of this book.)

   i)   _______________   v)   _______________

   ii) _______________   vi)   _______________

   iii) _______________   vii) _______________

   iv) _______________   viii) _______________

   Note: a maximum of six names are required to be entered because, according to the role of friendship, the number of people decreases as the relationship gets closer.

CHAPTER 3

YOUR FRIENDS AND COMPANIONS: WHO ARE THEY?

"Ye are my friends, if ye do whatsoever I command you. Henceforth I call you not servants, for the servant knoweth not what his Lord doeth: but I have called you friends; for all things that I have heard of my Father I have made known unto you. (**John 15:14-15**)

THE THIRD SPHERE or degree of human relationship, according to the model of Jesus in Luke Chapter 6, consists of those you call your friends and Companions. For Jesus, these were the 12 disciples that he chose from among the original 70 disciples.

All diagrams are original creation of the Author and may be used or reproduced by permission from the Author.

"[13] And when it was day, he called unto him **his disciples: and of them** *he chose twelve*, whom also he named apostles." (**Luke 6:12-19**).

Before I delve into this subject, I would want you to understand a few things about friendship.

Relationships affect your assignment in life, your assignment affects your destiny, and your destiny affects your legacy.

True friendship or relationship is far from the casual *"buddy-to-buddy"* system that we have gotten to know through social media and social networks. There is a special and ordained purpose to every relationship, and the purpose of a true relationship is to make you fruitful when you relate to the right person or people. God works with what is known as *"likeness."* For the Bible says in the beginning chapters of the book of Genesis (Genesis Chapter 1) that God created man in His own image and likeness. Have you ever wondered why God would create man in His 'likeness'? It is because He wanted to have a relationship with man. God needed something to relate to and so He made man not like a robot that one cannot reason with, but rather as a living soul that he can reason with and relate to.

You also must understand that not everyone you come across or you become acquainted with, should be in some sort of relationship with you or be brought into your inner circle of relationship.

You have to understand that relationships impact your assignment in life; your assignment in life impacts your destiny, and your destiny impacts your legacy.

Your Assignment—is what you are supposed to be doing in life. Your destiny is what you become as a result of your assignment and your legacy is what you leave behind for others to emulate.

Your Destiny—*is what you ultimately evolved into.* So, when people just want to hang out with you and eat food or just have fun, that's not what relationships are all about.

Your Legacy—is the positive impact that you leave behind after you have accomplished your life assignment and you are off the scene. "Off-the-scene" does not necessarily mean you are dead but also includes the period of time in your life when you no more have the strength or opportunity to continue with your particular assignment.

Your destiny is what you become, and your legacy is what you leave behind for others to emulate.

Be careful, therefore, that you guard your sphere of relationship away from the kind of people who are full of drama. The drama kings and drama queens are always ready to create a scene of real life drama around you, over the simplest situation they encounter in their life. They will just raise high your blood sugar level and leave you with no benefit from their being around you. As you get older and wiser, what you must guard against are people who are full of drama. This is because the older you get, the more difficult it becomes for you to be able to disentangle yourself from people who are full of drama.

Using the life of Abraham and his eventual separation from Terah and Lot as a perfect example, at times God may separate you from some friends and even some family members in order to bring you into your destiny. Don't be surprised when that happens to you, because although you meet together and interact as a church, family and for many other reasons, your destiny is not tied to their destiny. God had to separate Abraham from his father Terah and then from his nephew Lot just so God will bring him to the place where he could take full possession of the promises God had given him earlier in order to reach his destiny.

If you read the background story, you would notice that as long as Abraham had Terah and Lot with him, he could not settle. He was very unstable during that period of his life, and as a result, he had to move from one place to another. It wasn't until his father Terah died on the journey and his nephew Lot was separated from him that God showed up again to Abraham and said, *now I'm ready to take you to the next level where I have been wanting to bring you all this time.* Notice that it was after the separation from his father and his nephew that he was able to settle in order for Sarah to bear him Isaac—the child of promise. After that, God began to allow Abraham to prosper tremendously because he had now moved from the permissive will of God into the perfect will of God. The blessing never came before; it was only after.

As another example, Job's wife did not believe in Job nor in the God that Job served. Perhaps Job himself did not even know this until he was at his moment of loss. That was when his wife encouraged him to curse God and die (Job 2:9). Don't be surprised, because you can have people who are supposed to be close to you and yet they don't believe in you or in your vision. As a Pastor and Shepherd, I come across such people from time to time. Yes, I mean people in your inner circles. If your wife is not close to you, then who is or who will be? Did you marry the devil, or a woman you loved?

Jesus said to his disciples, ***"This is my commandment, that*** *ye love one another, as I have loved you. [13] Greater love hath no man than this, that a man lay down his life for his friends.*

14] Ye are my friends, if ye do whatsoever I command you.

15) Henceforth I call you not servants, for the servant knoweth not what his lord doeth: but I have called you friends, for all things that I have heard of my Father I have made known unto you.

16) Ye have not chosen me, but I have chosen you, and ordained you, that ye should go and bring forth fruit, and that your fruit should remain: that whatsoever ye shall ask of the Father in my name, he may give it you.

(John 15:12-16)

The Condition for Friendship.

In the previous chapter, I mentioned that true and healthy relationships should be based on understanding and not emotions. Notice from the Scripture quotation above that Jesus was giving His disciples the condition for His friendship with them. He said in Verse 14 that, **"Ye are my friends, if ye do whatsoever I command you."** The use of the word "if" makes this verse a conditional statement. It implies that He is giving them a condition which is also an agreement. It is an agreement in that as long as the disciples do whatsoever he commands them, he would have them as his friends.

Isn't it rather interesting to note that on the contrary, we are made to believe that love has no condition? But here we find Jesus, who himself is the embodiment of love, and yet he is giving his disciples a condition for His friendship with them.

One would say, "but I thought love has no conditions." What Jesus is saying to His disciples is certainly a condition or the terms to His relationship with his disciples. So then, where did we go wrong about that fact that relationships must be conditional and should be based on mutual agreement?

Also in Amos 3:3 is the following: ***"Can two walk together, except they agree?"***

Agreement means coming into an understanding with someone pertaining to a particular issue. So here again, for two people to be able to meaningfully relate one to another, there should be an agreement. Therefore, be careful about the people who think their friendship with you should be based on emotions and hence they clamor around you like emotional "roller-coasters."

Your Friends and Companions: Who are They?

One of the trademarks of this generation is our carelessness in the use of words. We have become a generation of people who tend to trivialize words so much that at times we use some words to refer to things that we know do not merit the meaning of those words. We go about expressing our love for things that we know can't reciprocate that love to us. As an example, at times you would hear people expressing their love for candies or other items that cannot love them back instead of simply saying that they like them. It's amazing we "love" these things instead of "like" them.

Have you ever had any of the things you claim to love, love you back in any form or manner? Most often, people apply the same behavior towards the people they casually meet. They meet someone on the train or bus at one time and when they see him or her on another occasion, they claim they know them. Or they speak with someone once or twice and they begin to call them their friend. But who are those who should really deserve to be called friends?

As mentioned earlier in this chapter, the third degree or sphere of relationship are your friends and companions. As a child of God, this group of people should be those you walk closely with as you walk with Christ. These are the people to whom you can correctly apply the word "friend." Again, please be careful not to put the word friend to the crowd or even your colleagues and associates. Otherwise you are going to be greatly disappointed down the line.

In Jesus' model of relationship, His sphere of friends and companions were not the multitudes of people who followed Him. They were not the 58 plus disciples who left after he chose the 12 Apostles. Rather, those he called friends were the 12 disciples who later became known as the Apostles of the Lamb and who he drew closer to himself during the span of his earthly ministry. As mentioned earlier, note that this number is reduced from the countless crowds of people, to the 70 disciples, to the 12 disciples and finally to the 3 inner core confidants known as Peter, James and John. The closer the relationship gets, the lesser the number becomes. This is because relationships draw virtue, time, energy, and attention out of you. Therefore, a word of caution is, be careful you are not spending all the energy you have in your personal "energy bank" on people who are far off and do not have your well-being at heart.

As a child of God, your friends or companions should be simply people who can walk with you, as you walk with God.

The Apostle Paul puts it in this way, *"Learn of me, as I learn of Christ,"* or *"follow me as I follow after Christ."* What you ought to understand is that this kind of relationship is not for everyone you come across because this type of relationship is not superficial. It draws virtue out of you. True friendship and companionship is energy consuming; it demands your time, your attention, your affection and your energy. This is heavy stuff and is not for everyone you come across.

In researching the subject of relationships, and the meaning of the word *"companion,"* I looked for the *etymology* or the *true historic origin of the word "companion"* and I found out that it comes from the old English word: **Com** which means **"With"** and ***panis*** (pronounced as paa-ins) which means *"**bread**."* So the two words, when put together, become *Com-panis* in the (Greek) and compagnon (French) and companion (English). Hence the word "companion" means "One who shares the same bread with you" or one who eats the same diet.

I find this to be very interesting because it is exactly in line with the admonishment of the Bible when it instructs us not to be equally yoked with unbelievers. Applying the meaning of the word companion to it, this implies that since we do not eat the same spiritual bread as unbelievers, they should not have the privilege to be called our companions.

So, there is a problem when the people you happen to call your friends or best friends are those who don't eat the same spiritual bread as you. How can you, a child of God, share closeness and friendship with people who eat the bread of malice, lasciviousness, lies, hatred, jealousy, and worldliness? Can't you see that something is just not right with some of the associations you may have? Can't you see that having people who eat the bread of malice, lasciviousness, lies, hatred, jealousy, and worldliness in your relationship closet can be a danger to your spiritual growth in the Lord? I challenge you to re-examine the kind of people you have in your relationship closet and to trim it down to those who share the same spiritual bread, virtues and values as you do.

1. The meaning of "Bread" in the Bible.

Bread in the Bible signifies revelation. Therefore, your companions then should be people who share the same spiritual diet or revelation as you do. And you should know by now that this can't be just any- and everybody. That's why the Apostle Paul in Ephesians 5:15 admonishes us to, ***"See then that ye walk circumspectly, not as fools, but as wise."***

Circumspectly is an old English word which simply means to be watchful and discreet. It also means to be cautious or prudent. Finally, it means to consider well. What this means is that the kind of people you walk with and call your friends and companions should be well considered by you before you even choose them as friends. If you fail to prepare in choosing your friends, it means you are preparing for failure.

True friendship draws virtue out of you because it demands your time, your attention, your affection and your energy.

2. Bread in the Bible also signifies "Life."

That's why when Jesus declared boldly in Matthew Chapter 6, that He is the bread of life and they didn't understand Him, they were about to stone Him. If bread signifies life, then your companions should be those that you share the same spiritual life with. Again, that can't be just any- and everybody. Furthermore, in my research, I have found that the Hebrew word for "Companion" is the word "raw-aw" which means to graze together, which also points to eating together of the same foods like a flock of sheep grazing together on a grassland.

In conclusion to this chapter, I would like to dwell on a Scripture in Proverbs 27:6 which reads, ***"Faithful are the wounds of a friend, but the kisses of an enemy are deceitful."***

That is why the only people you should allow to cut you or criticize you are your true friends and companions. Close your ears to people who are afar off in the "crowds" and yet try to criticize you for every move you make. They don't have the right to criticize you because they are not within the sphere of people who have your well-being at heart. If you allow them to cut you (not literally), chances are that they will want to kill you.

However, when a true friend cuts you, they cut you in order to heal you. That's why the writer in the book of Proverbs says, "Faithful are the wounds of a friend," because when a friend inflicts wounds, they do so with your well-being in mind; although they are cutting you, they could remove that thorn in your flesh. They do it with caution in order not to hurt you but rather to help you heal because they are friends. On the other hand, if you give an enemy the chance to remove the same thorn in your flesh, before you know it, they are cutting deep into your flesh in order to damage some nerves and eventually incapacitate you or even kill you. So, the writer cautions us to watch the kisses of an enemy because they are deceitful.

'Food-For-Thought'
Worksheet for Chapter 3

The S.W.A.G Test.

When identifying who your friends should be, the first criteria to consider is; are the people you call friends

<u>SMART</u>,

<u>WISE</u>,

<u>AMICABLE</u>,

<u>GODLY?</u>

<u>SMART</u>—*"Behold, I send you forth as sheep in the midst of wolves; be ye therefore smart as serpents, and harmless as doves." (Matthew 10:16)*

<u>WISE</u>—*"He that walketh with wise men shall be wise: but a companion of fools shall be destroyed." (Proverbs 13:20).*

<u>AMICABLE</u>—*"As we have the opportunity, let us do good unto all men, and especially toward them that are of the household of the faith." (Galatians 6:10)*

<u>GODLY</u>—*"Be not deceived, ungodly companionship corrupt good morals." (I Corinthians 15:33)*

1. List three characteristics associated with the kind of people you should call your friends or companions.

    i. ____

    ii. ____

    iii. ____

2. List at least 4 established boundaries by which your friendship is guided.

    i. ____

    ii. ____

    iii. ____

    iv. ____

3. As a person of faith, how many of the above-established boundaries are spiritually related.

4. Are you experiencing any spiritual boost from being friends with those whom you call your "friends?"

5. If your answer is YES:

    i. In what way are they positively influencing your life?

    ii. In what way are you positively influencing their life?

6. Do the people you call your friends and companions share the same values, philosophy and ideology of life as you do?

Yes? OR No?

   i. If your answer to the above questions is "No" then the smart and wise action to take is to re-assess your friendship closet and cut off your association with those who do not share your spiritual and moral values.

7. List four people in your life that you can truly refer to as your friends and companions. Think carefully about it and ensure that the names you jot down below are not people who fall within your first or second sphere of relationship. In other words, ensure they are neither in the crowds of people you relate with casually nor people that you relate with functionally because of work, school, business etc.

(Refer to shaded portion of diagram below and the various characteristics of friends and companions mentioned throughout the third chapter of this book)

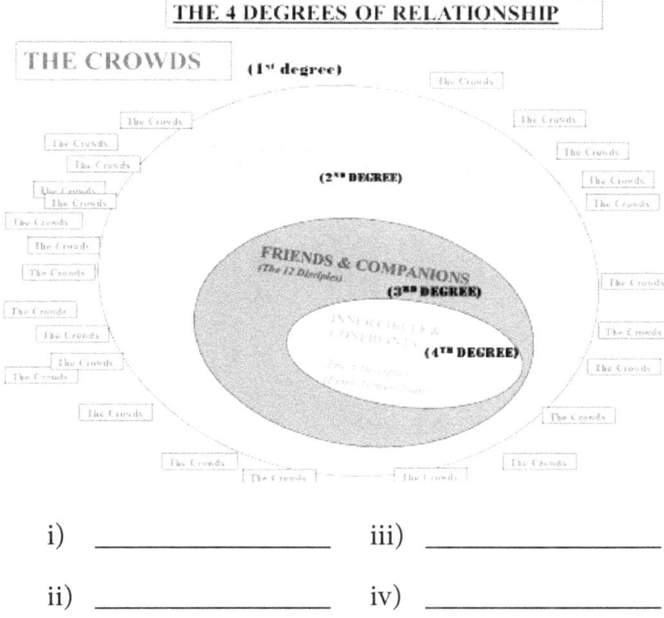

i) ______________   iii) ______________

ii) ______________   iv) ______________

Note a maximum of four names are required to be entered because, according to the role of friendship, the number of people decreases as the relationship gets closer.

CHAPTER 4

INNER CIRCLE OF FRIENDS
& CONFIDANTS

THE 4TH DEGREE of relationship in your sphere or relationships are your inner circle of friends. To be exact, these are the people you can call your confidants. The ones you share your heart with, the deep things that you would not share with just anyone. They are those people in your life who are there to stay. These are the people who have your well-being at heart and love you to death. Their love for you is unconditional.

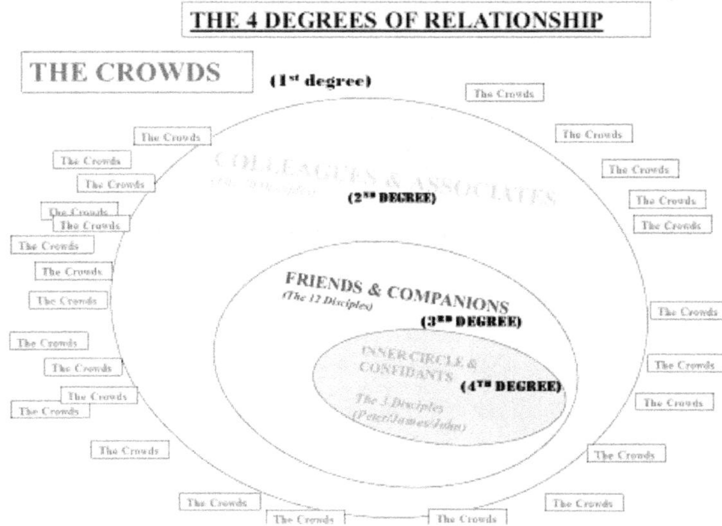

All diagrams are original creation of the Author and may be used or reproduced by permission from the Author.

These people are into you whether you are up or down. They are with you for the long haul. God forbid, should you get into trouble, they will come and see you in the jail house. You may be sick in the hospital and doctors don't want people to come close to you because of the nature of sickness, yet they will still find their way to draw close to you.

They are around you not for any personal gain or anything they can get from you, but rather because they mean you well. Listen to me friend, these kinds of people are hard to come by, but they are the kind of people you need in your life, not the crowds. You may never reach your fullest potential until you find who your confidants are. That's how important they are to your life.

You cannot be a "David" until you find your "Jonathan" in life.

The above statement is true because, like David, you were raised outside the gates of the palace, but God is going to cause you to reach over the wall into the Palace, through a Jonathan. Even when you get to the palace, you will still need a Jonathan to caution you and protect you from the fury of a King Saul if you are ever going to survive and stay alive in the palace.

You've got to have somebody who can feed you, so you can feed others, and these are your confidants and people in your inner circle. Somebody who can pour into you, so you will be able to pour into others and this task can be accomplished only through your confidants. Notice that, unlike the crowds and the colleagues or associates, your confidants are very few in number and hard to come by. For some it may even be one person in your life. For others, it may be two or three at most, but the fewer they are, the better. Looking at the model of Jesus as an example, His inner circle was these three men: Peter, James and John. Later in this chapter, I will delve into the virtues and characteristics that these three men brought to their association with Jesus. They were men of great virtue although what they contributed to their relationship with Jesus was totally different, one from the other.

....

Note that your inner circle of friends and confidants cannot be many because this level or sphere of relationship is so close that it will draw from you energy, virtue, time, attention, and much sacrifice.

....

Be prepared because they will get into your business and they will tell you frankly when you are wrong. But they are not doing so to hurt you; rather they heal you and strengthen you.

In the inner circle of Jesus, the Bible says He chooses Peter, also known as Simon who is the son of Jona, and then he chooses James and John, the two Sons of Zebedee and draws these men much closer to himself than the remaining 9 disciples. If you watch carefully, you will notice that Jesus always took along Peter, James and John during very critical and crucial moments in His life.

As examples, notice that:

1. In the Mt. of Transfiguration (Matt 17:1) Jesus took with him Peter, James and John.

2. In the garden of Gethsemane, (Mark 14:33) Jesus took with him all the 12 disciples but drew Peter, James and John further with him into the garden to prayer while the remaining 9 were left behind.

3. In the House of Simon Peter where Jesus healed Peter's mother-in-law of fever, (Mark 1:29) Jesus took with him, Peter, James, and John. This time around however, Andrew came along with the three

men because Andrew was the brother of Peter, and since Jesus was visiting with their family, it was just proper that he accompanied them.

4. Going to the house of Jairus, Jesus knew ahead of time what he was up against (that is a house full of scorners and unbelievers). So here again, like other times, Jesus took along with Him Peter, James, and John. (Mark 5:35-40)

5. Besides the four Gospels, in the Epistles, further mention was made in Galatians 2:9 of Peter, James and John as the pillars of the Church. This is because these three men had some unique virtues and qualities that the others did not have.

PETER

Starting with Peter, in all catalogues of the apostles, Peter stands at the head. He is a man full of fire and energy, the son of Jonah, who is to become a rock, a pillar, and the spokesman of the apostolic circle. Peter is a man with a fiery spirit, ever ready for combat. He represents the first quality of friendship because Peter is bold, but also honest in his dealings with people. This is a quality of friendship that one needs in their life because it is this quality that keeps us accountable. These people are in your life to bring checks and balances into your life, so be careful not to drive them away. You would be digging your own grave so to speak, if you surround yourself with "yes men." By that, I mean people who are not bold enough to point out to you when you are on the wrong path or people who would not give you their honest opinion because they are afraid they will fall out of favor with you.

If you look carefully, you will find out that among all the 12 disciples of Jesus that he called out of the 70, only Peter had the boldness to say things that the others wanted to say but could not. As a matter of fact, almost all the turbulence among the 12 disciples always came from Peter. Let me share with you a few examples of occasions when Peter clearly stood out as the boldest among all the other disciples of Jesus.

Examples:

1. **In John 6:68** when other disciples turned their back on Jesus and began to walk away from Him, Jesus asked the remaining disciples, "Will ye also go?" While all the other 11 disciples were quiet, it was Peter who responded boldly and said, "To whom shall we go, Lord, for You have the words of eternal life and we believe."

2. **In Matt 18:21**, Peter posed the question about "How many times one should forgive his brother when they sin against him," perhaps because Peter could not tolerate someone who might have been bordering him anymore.

3. **In Matt 19:27**, Peter posed the bold and difficult question to Jesus. ***"What do we get after we have left all and followed you?"*** In other words, what's in it for us after leaving our various professions as fishermen (Peter, James and John), tax collector (Matthew), Physician (Luke), political activist (Simon the Zealot) and the others who were of different lines of profession to follow Jesus? Was this a question that any of the other disciples may

have wanted to ask? Certainly yes, but were any of the others bold enough to ask such a sensitive question? No, not at all, except Peter.

4. **In Luke 8:45**, Peter responded when Jesus asked the disciples about who it was that might have touched Him in the crowd while He was on His way to Jairus' house to heal Jairus' daughter.

5. **In John 13:8**, while Jesus was at the dinner table with his disciples during the Last Supper, while the others just went with the flow, it was Peter who resisted Jesus' washing of his feet because he claimed that Jesus was their master and hence not supposed to wash his feet. Jesus responded and said to Peter, "If I wash thee not, ye shall have no part with me"

6. **In John 13:24,** Peter beckoned John to ask Jesus who is it that was to betray Him.

7. **In Matthew 14:28** during the storm, when Jesus walked on water, it was Peter who was bold enough to say to Jesus, ***"Lord if it be Thou, bid me to come unto Thee on the water,"*** and boldly Peter began to walk on the waters immediately after Jesus had bid him to come. Notice that although this was a great and notable miracle, there is a caveat here. That is, although Peter physically walked on the water, he was only able to do that because he walked on the word Christ gave him. If he did not fix his eyes on the word Jesus gave him, he couldn't have been able to walk on the water. So, notice that the moment Peter took his eyes off the word that was given to him by Jesus, and began to focus on the

impossibility of walking on the surface of water, he began to sink.

....

As long as you fix your eyes upon the words of Jesus, you will be sustained above your storms; however, the moment you begin to consider the impossibilities of your circumstances, instead of the greatness of God's power, you will begin to sink in the face of your storms.

....

As an illustration, the story was told of a mammal that had to cross from one side of a river to the other side in order to escape death. Because it could not swim across, it was left without any hope of survival until two birds flew by and decided to offer their help to get the mammal across the river. The two birds therefore decided to hold the ends of a piece of stick with their beaks and the mammal cling to the middle of the stick with its mouth while they flew it across the river. So, while the two birds were in the air with the mammal clung to the middle of the stick, a third bird flew past them and to its amusement, saw the mammal in the air together with the two birds. And the third bird said to the mammal, "You must be such a wonderful mammal to be able to fly at such a high altitude without wings." Upon hearing these words of praise, the mammal became so proud and for a moment, it forgot that it was only able to be in the air at such altitude because it was being supported by holding on to the middle of a stick with its mouth whiles being flown by two birds. As soon as the mammal attempted to open its mouth and to let the third bird know how wonderful and skillful it was, it fell off the stick and plunged to its death in the middle of the river.

This illustration is just like Peter accomplishing what seemed to be the impossibility of walking on water. His downfall came when he took his eyes off the words of Jesus and began to focus on himself and the impossible circumstance around him. It was also a picture of the believer in Christ Jesus. This is exactly what happens to the children of God when we take our eyes off the word of God and begin to trust in ourselves instead of the grace of God.

8. Lastly, in the 16th Chapter of Matthew's gospel, it is recorded that Jesus took His disciples to a place called Caesarea Philippi which was noted to be the center of idol worship. It was in this stronghold of satanic forces where Jesus asked His disciples what public opinion and also their opinion of Him was. ***"Who do you say that I, the Son of man, am?"*** Notice that the eleven Disciples couldn't answer the question but when Jesus asked earlier about who others said He was, they were quick to answer that, "some say Thou art Elias and others say Thou art Jeremias or one of the Prophets." However, when

Jesus sought their personal opinion of Him, they were all afraid to answer. Here again like other times, it was Peter who was bold enough to answer Jesus by saying: ***"Thou art the Christ, the Son of the living God."*** **(Matt. 16:16).** The implication here is that people will easily tell you what others are saying about you but only a few have a revelation about who you are.

Jesus then responded and said to Peter, ***[18] And I say also unto thee, that thou art Peter, and upon this rock I will build my church, and the gates of hell shall not prevail against it.***

Therefore, Simon Peter, in answering Jesus' question, correctly received a great commendation from Jesus. However, it is interesting what happened next in the same chapter between Jesus and Peter immediately after receiving this great commendation from his master Jesus. Jesus then awarded Peter with the keys of the Kingdom when He said unto Him in Verse 19, ***"And I will give unto thee the keys of the kingdom of heaven: and whatsoever thou shalt bind on earth shall be bound in heaven: and whatsoever thou shalt loose on earth shall be loosed in heaven."***

....

Jesus gave Peter the keys because when you have people in your life who are bold and honest, to such people goes the keys to your life.

....

Keys by their nature give access. Therefore, you cannot give people who are neither bold nor honest access to the intimate things and issues of your life. The best they would do would be to ruin your life if you ever granted them such access into your life.

The danger here with many people is that they have given the wrong people the keys to their lives and as such they are being destroyed by people. Yet they keep going back to them for pity. You cannot put the keys to your life into the hands of people who are in the crowd, and neither is it wise to do so with people who are just your associates because they, not knowing what to do with it, would end up ruining your life, hope, dreams and aspirations. Quit the "pity-party" and begin to think about inviting into your life people ordained by God to impact your life positively.

Therefore, after such a great commendation and with the keys of the Kingdom now jingling in the hands of Peter, Jesus now felt comfortable enough to announce to the disciples His plans to head towards Jerusalem and eventually towards His ultimate death on the cross. It is interesting to note from the verses 21–23 of Matthew 16, what happened after this announcement.

Matthew 16:21-23 *"From that time forth began Jesus to shew unto his disciples, how that he must go unto Jerusalem, and suffer many things of the elders and chief priests and scribes, and be killed, and be raised again the third day."*

This story and dialogue between Jesus and Peter, in the presence of the other disciples, is very interesting because a few moments after Jesus had commended Peter, Jesus went on to announce his eminent departure through the death on the cross. In Verse 22, we are told that: *[22] "Then Peter took Him, and began to rebuke Him, saying, be it far from Thee, Lord: this shall not be unto Thee."*

That is unimaginable that Peter would take his master Jesus aside and begin to rebuke Him as one would do to an unruly child. That's totally unbelievable. However, Peter did it because it showed how bold Peter was compared to the other disciples.

Immediately following Peter's rebuke, Jesus now looks into the face of the same person (Peter) who he commended a few moments ago and rebuked him with a stern rebuke by referring to him as Satan. *[23] But he turned, and said unto Peter, get thee behind me, Satan: thou art an offence unto me: for thou savourest not the things that be of God, but those that be of men.*

Jesus looks one of His closest companions in the face and rebukes him by saying, *"Get behind me, Satan."* Could you believe that? The same companion that Jesus commended a little while before in the presence of the other 11 disciples, but now rebukes sharply. Do you have friends like that who can boldly correct you and vice-versa and everything would still be fine between you both?

If it were to be some of us, this would have been the breaking point of our relationship with one another. For many, this event would have been enough to get them packing their bags to leave. That is when you would hear statements like: "I feel the Lord is leading me in a different direction and so I can no more work together in the ministry with you". Does this statement sound familiar? Can you identify it with any circumstances in your life where people had turned their backs on you and parted from you simply because they did not agree with you pertaining to some issue or matter? As a Pastor, I have had several experiences which led to people parting ways with me. Frankly speaking, those moments can be painful. But again, they are the moments in life that give you the opportunity to reassess the caliber of people you have around you.

If many were in the shoes of Peter, they would have said to Jesus, "How dare you speak to me like that and embarrass me in front of the other 11 disciples?" Do you have friends like Jesus and Peter whom you can correct and who can also boldly correct you and everything will still be cool between both of you? As the saying goes, *"It takes iron to sharpen an iron."* Hence having such bold and honest friends as Peter in your life is a great blessing. Such friends are hard to come by, so make sure you keep them when they come your way. They are bold and can point out your mistakes to you, but at the same time, they are honest in that they are not doing it to belittle you and make you feel like you are a failure.

All these back and forth rebukes between Jesus and Peter, happened in Chapter 16 of Matthew's gospel. Then in the next chapter that immediately follows (Matthew 17), we see where Jesus is taking them, His closest companions Peter, James and John, along with him to the mountain where He would be transfigured. Many people who are unforgiving would have followed Jesus up into the mountain rumbling about how He had rebuked them and did not apologize but yet He was taking them along to the mountain. However, Peter went up with him silently without hesitation, and at the end of the experience on the mountain, he was rather thankful for being in the company of Jesus. Look at Peter's remarks after he had followed Jesus to the mountain of transfiguration when he saw the glory of God.

Matthew 17:1-4 (KJV) *"And after six days Jesus taketh Peter, James, and John his brother, and bringeth them up into a high mountain apart, [2] And was transfigured before them: and his face did shine as the sun, and his raiment was white as the light. [3] And, behold, there appeared unto* *them Moses and Elias talking with him. [4]* **Then answered Peter, and said unto Jesus, Lord, it is good for us to be here . . . ."**

In Verse 4, after the Mount of Transfiguration experience, Peter was grateful enough to say to Jesus, "Lord, it is good for us to be here." Friends in your lives like Peter who are bold and honest keep you accountable. Hence if you don't have friends like that, it's about time you pray to God for one.

JOHN

The virtues of the disciple John represent the second quality of friendship. While most of the action and turbulence among the 12 disciples comes from Peter, John on the other hand is more interesting because he represents the loving, caring and loyal friend. As he is patient in enduring, he represents the heart of Jesus' sphere or circle of relationship with the disciples. When Jesus died, after the third day it was told to the disciples that Jesus had arisen from the dead (**John 20:3-4**) and John and Peter began to run to the tomb to see for themselves if what they heard was true. The Bible records that John outran Peter. The spiritual implication here is that,

Those who love you will always out-distance those who know you.

Since the "Johns" in your life are loving and loyal, what they bring into your life is that they keep you relationally connected.

At the dinner table during the last supper, when Jesus said to His disciples, *"One of you is going to betray me,"* Peter requested that John ask Jesus who it is that is going to betray Him and while having his head on Jesus' bosom John said softly to the Lord *"who is it Lord,"* **(John 13:21-25)**. This is a beautiful story because as bold as Peter was, why would he not ask the Lord Jesus himself but had to ask through John? Peter had to ask through John not because he lacked the boldness to do so, because obviously Peter was the boldest among all the 12 disciples. He had to ask through John, since John was more loving and more caring. This meant it would be easier for John to reach the heart of Jesus than Peter could. People who are more loving and caring like John are usually more capable of touching the hearts of others easier and faster than people who are simply bold and frank like Peter.

Listen to me, Friend. People who love you and care about you like John are the ones you should give your heart to, not the people in the crowds. This is because the "Johns" in your life are the kind of people who have their ears to your pulse. They know and understand your heartbeat and your rhythm in life. While you may be able to hide your emotions about some unpleasant feeling from others, such people can see you and immediately know that something is going on in your life. It is so sad that too many people have given their hearts to people who are in the crowd and as a result, they are stomping all over their heart, causing them to bleed internally, figuratively speaking.

If you are truthful with yourself, some of you are hurting emotionally because of the unhealthy friendship and relationships that you may have gone through in the past or are going through in your life now.

Do not give your heart to people who do not have their ears to your heart-beat. They will never understand you because they do not understand your rhythm in life.

Do you have people around you who love you even in your lowest times? They are the "Johns." Even when you mess up and their association with you may cause them to be indicted, they will still be around you. Among all the disciples of Jesus, none went so far as John would go during the crucifixion of our Lord Jesus. At the cross, John was the only disciple among all the 12 who was found closest in proximity to the cross of Jesus Christ. While all the others scattered for fear of the Jews and Roman Soldiers and wouldn't come near, John was right there, at least close enough for Jesus to be able to look down on him even with his corroded vision from blood streaming down from the crown of thrones that the Roman soldiers forced on his head.

No wonder John was the one to whom Jesus entrusted the care of His mother, Mary. Jesus said to John and to Mary, probably the only ones close enough to the cross, ***"Woman, behold thy son, and son, behold thy mother."*** John, knowing the heartbeat and rhythm of his Master and friend, clearly understood what Jesus meant by that statement and so the Bible says that John took Mary, the mother of Jesus, unto his own home to be with him. **(John19:27)**

If you want to know where Peter, the boldest among the disciples was, see what Mark's account of the gospel tells us about that. ***Mark 14:54*** tells us that ***"Peter followed Him but*** *from afar off."* So, while Peter followed on from afar and the other disciples were "missing in action," John was the only one who was right there beside Mary, the mother of Jesus. That is how far the "Johns" in your life will go for your sake, because their attachment to you is not for any personal gain but simply their love and care for your well-being. Please remember that in your moments of joy and elation, these are the people who deserve a dance with you.

Therefore, while Jesus would give Peter the Keys to the Kingdom because he was bold and honest, Jesus on the other hand gave John his heart because he was loving and caring. So, to Peter went the keys and to John went the heart. No wonder Jesus permitted John, the beloved disciple, to live longer than the other two disciples who made up his inner core of friends. Whiles the other two (Peter and James) died as martyrs of the faith, Jesus allowed John to be the only one among the three to die a natural death. **Acts 12:2** tells us that James was killed by the sword and Church History tells us that Peter was hanged up-side-down at his own request because he found himself not worthy to die in the same manner as his Lord and Master Jesus was hanged.

Jesus allowed John to live long enough to write part of the gospels, part of the epistles as well as the book of the last thing (the book of the revelations of our Lord Jesus Christ). Among the countless people that Jesus became acquainted with, John was the only one to be referred to in the gospel as the disciple whom Jesus loved because of how loving and caring he was.

Also, according to John 21:7, when Jesus resurrected from the dead after the third day and showed up at the shores, Peter could not recognize Him. He thought he was a stranger. It was John who immediately identified Jesus upon seeing Him and told Peter and the others that it was the Lord. When you live with people close enough for a time, their presence rubs off on you. You begin to reason like them, think like them, act like them and even speak like them. That's why it's very important to be mindful of who you hang out with. Sooner or later you would either act like them or talk like them. Even if you don't act or talk like them, people will judge you with their character as a result of your association with them.

JAMES

The disciple, James, represents the third quality or virtue of friendship. Throughout the gospels, one would notice that James doesn't say much but he is selected together with Peter and John every time a critical situation arises. When it was time to go to Jairus' house in Mark 5, Jesus took with him Peter, John and James. When it was time to go to the Mount of Transfiguration, Jesus took along with him Peter, John and James. When it was time to travail in prayer in the garden of Gethsemane, Jesus left the 9 disciples and he took with him Peter, John and James. Here we see that James was always part of Jesus' inner circle of confidants and yet James says absolutely nothing in the gospels. It is interesting to note that not a single word comes out of James' mouth in the account of the gospels and yet he was always chosen alongside Peter and John to be part of Jesus' inner circle.

Whiles Peter, John and a few other disciples contributed to the writing of the gospels, there exists no gospel according to James, nor did we read of any contribution in any of the gospels made by James, yet he is one of the three disciples who are closest to Jesus. Notice that nothing was said in the gospels about James or from James, until in the book of Acts where he is made a Bishop of the Church.

The question therefore is, how come James is always named

among Jesus' inner circle of friends or disciples and yet not much is heard from James? The "James" people are the kind of friends in your life who don't say much because by their nature, they are people of few words. Nevertheless, they are always present. You can count on them to be by your side in moments of rejoicing, pain, or sorrow and although they will be present, yet they do not utter many words. They are *silent but always present.* These are friends who are with you but their relationship with you is not in words but rather in their presence.

According to Job 2:11-13, the friends of Job (Eliphaz the Temanite, Bildad the Shuhite, and Zophar the Naamathite) came purposely to comfort Job when they heard of the calamities that had befallen him. However, it is very interesting to note how they went about it. Let's see how **Job 2:11-13** describes their actions as they came to comfort Job:

"Now when Job's three friends heard of all this evil that was come upon him, they came everyone from his own place, Eliphaz the Temanite, and Bildad the Shuhite, and Zophar the Naamathite: for they had made an appointment together to come to mourn with him and to comfort him. [12] And when they lifted up their eyes afar off, and knew him not, they lifted up their voice, and wept, and they rent everyone his mantle, and sprinkled dust upon their heads toward heaven. [13] So they sat down with him upon the ground seven days and seven nights, and none spake a word unto him: for they saw that his grief was very great."

Notice from the passage above that they came and sat with Job for seven days and seven nights and yet they did not utter a single word to Job. They did not say a word to him, but rather, whatever situation they met him in, they sat in it with him. So, they came to see Job in sackcloth and they also put on sackcloth. They saw him with ashes upon his head as a sign of grief and deep sorrow and they also put ashes upon their heads. They came to see Job rent his garment and so did they. They came to see Job sitting upon the ground and so did they together with him. For a period of seven days and seven nights, they uttered not a word to their friend Job. Their action is amazing because true friends are those who will embrace and join you in whatever situation they find you in, without saying a word.

> **There are situations in life where words are insufficient to bring comfort, as one's presence would do.**

Be careful not to push the "James" in your life away simply because you don't hear enough words from them. Remember that their relationship with you is not in words but rather in their presence.

Being present but silent is a virtue that is needed in a relationship, especially under circumstances of grief and deep sorrow. There are certain situations in life that you may find yourself in, where words alone are not enough or sufficient to bring healing and comfort. In those moments and under such circumstances, what you need is not people who will come around and try to make up or formulate words, but rather, faithful friends who will come and sit with you during your afflictions and trouble.

Unlike the "Peters" who are bold and honest, and the

"Johns" who are loving and caring, the "James" in your sphere of relationship bring trust into your life and that helps to boost your confidence and gives you strength to bear your pain and sorrows.

I remember vividly a few years ago when my wife was suddenly diagnosed with a type of neurological condition that totally incapacitated the functions of the muscles in her body and at times led to short breath and other serious and life threatening medical crises. It was just about seven years into our marriage and our three children were very young at the time. The seriousness of the condition, coupled with the sudden emergency brought so much shock to me as a young husband that I didn't know how to handle or cope with the situation. I remember in those days, I would visit my wife at the hospital and stay at her bedside for long periods without being able to find words to express how I was feeling about the whole situation. Although what I would have loved to do was to encourage her with strong words that would elevate her faith, in my grief, I couldn't find words to utter about her condition. However, I was always present daily at her bedside no matter how tired my workday had been.

Such was James' relationship with Jesus. He was always present with Jesus during every critical moment of His life, but his presence was not necessarily expressed in words. This is a great virtue that is lacking in many relationships because at times people try to make up words when comforting friends or loved ones who are in grief. But words alone are at times not enough to smooth the pain and deep sorrow of people going through grief.

So again, while Jesus would give Peter the Keys to the Kingdom because he was bold and honest, and John His heart because he was loving and caring, Jesus on the other hand, gave

James His trust because he was always loyal and present with Him. Therefore, in conclusion . . .

To Peter goes the KEYS,

To John goes the HEART,

To James goes the TRUST.

O how beautiful are the virtues of these three men who were with Jesus and who became the closest to Him among all the other disciples.

....

These three men teaches us that relationships are supposed to be covenantal, even though the world has taken it to a casual level and have misused and abused it as a tool for socializing.

....

These three men (Peter, James and John) represent God's checks and balances in your relationships and lives because at the end of the day, you need someone who is bold and honest enough to tell you when you are wrong and you can also correct them without any animosity. These are the "Peters" in your life. Someone who really and truly loves and cares about you, whether you are up or down. Whether you are on your mountaintop or down below in your valley. Whether you are in your season of winning or in your season of losing. These are the "Johns."

Finally, you need in your sphere of relationships someone

who, when you look around, will always be there with you in your troubles. They are silent but present. These are the "James" in your life. **Proverbs 18:24** declares that, ***"A man that hath friends must shew himself friendly; there is a friend that sticketh closer than a brother."***

'Food-For-Thought'

Worksheet for Chapter 4

The S.W.A.G Test. (Continued)

Are the People you call Friends **SMART, WISE, AMICABLE & GODLY?**

1. If you are asked to name one or two people at most whom you confide in and share the most personal issues in your life with, who would those two people be?

2. How do you know who in your life is worth that privilege?

   See a few factors to consider when deciding:

   i. Do they love you unconditionally and have your well-being at heart?

   ii. Do they show care for you and are present whether you are going through your high or low seasons in life?

   iii. Are they the type of people who will still associate themselves with you when you mess up or God forbid, when you find yourself in some sort of trouble even if their association with you might have serious repercussions for them?

   iv. Are they the type who would boldly but positively criticize you when they realize you are heading towards the wrong path, and yet love you despite their criticism of you or your actions?

3. If you answered "Yes" to all the questions in #2 above, then this person is worth the privilege of being called your Confidant or among your inner circle of Friends.

4. If your answer to any of the questions in #2 above is "No," then begin to re-consider admitting such person(s) into your sphere of intimacy and affording them the privilege they do not deserve in your life.

5. As relationships or friendships get closer and more intimate, the number decreases. Hence as a word of caution, be careful and mindful to deliberately keep the numbers in your intimate sphere of friendship to the minimum. As a godly guide, Jesus had three persons within his intimate sphere of friendship, namely Peter, James and John. How many can you handle if Jesus thought it wise to limit the number to three?

6. List a couple of people that you can truly refer to as your inner circle of friends and confidants. Think carefully about it and ensure that the names you select below are not people who fall within your first three spheres of relationship.

   (Refer to shaded portion of diagram at the beginning of this chapter and the various characteristics of inner circle of friends and confidants mentioned throughout the fourth chapter of this book)

i.   _____________________________________

ii.   _____________________________________

Note: A maximum of two names are required to be entered because, according to the role of friendship, the number of people decreases as the relationship gets closer and more intimate.

CHAPTER 5

THE 5 DYNAMICS OF FRIENDSHIP (THE 5 "C's" OF FRIENDSHIP)

I N THIS CHAPTER, I will delve into the five dynamics of true friends. True and genuine friends will comfort you, cover you, carry you, caution you and finally care about you. This is what I have termed the five "C's" of friendship because every one of these qualities begins with the letter C. Before I discuss the subject of this chapter in more depth, I would like to weigh-in on a few of the Bible characters that have already been referenced, either in depth, or in passing in the previous chapters.

THE "PETERS"

You have to understand that although some friends may tend to be fuzzy around you, they are so only because they mean you well and would like to see you succeed in life. My counsel to you here is be careful not to drive them away simply because of their behavior, since they have your well-being at heart.

Consider, for instance the fact that among all the 12 disciples who were with Jesus, none was more irritable than Peter, none more turbulent than Peter, and none more provocative than Peter. However, when it came to protecting his master Jesus, *none among the 12 was more willing to cut ears off in defense of his master the way Peter did.*

People like Peter who are in your life or your personal sphere of relationship may get on your case at times. They may even rebuke you like Peter boldly did to Jesus, yet they still have your well-being at heart. The only reason Peter would draw a sword and cut off the ears of one of the people who came to arrest Jesus in the garden was because he didn't want them to do any harm to Jesus although he did not have a clear picture of the fact that Jesus must go to the cross to be slain as the sacrificial Lamb of God.

However, the fact still remains that Peter, besides all the other disciples, was willing to fight in defense of his master. Have you ever had people in your life who will criticize you to the "t" because they would like to see to it that all your "i's" are dotted and all your "t's" are crossed in whatever endeavors you undertake? Don't cast such people away from your life because they are there in your life for your own good.

THE "THOMASES"

There is a beautiful piece of Scripture in **Mark 3:14** which reads, ***"And he ordained twelve, that they should be with him, and that he might send them forth to preach."***

However, the truth remains that some might be with you and yet doubt you. These are the *"Thomases"* you have in your life. Just as I mentioned earlier about the "Peters," be careful not to cast the *"Thomases"* in your life away. If you do, it will be like throwing the baby away together with the bath water, because you may still need them down the line. That's why, although Jesus knew what was in Thomas, He never alienated him from the other eleven Disciples and so was Judas. With the Thomases, this is how the dynamics of friendship goes. When you try to sell your dream and vision to them, they may not object. Yet within them is doubt as to whether that dream or vision would ever materialize. Although they don't mean any harm to you as a person, you cannot count on them to boost your spirit or serve as an encouragement to you.

Since they cannot believe in your dreams, they would usually stay on the sidelines as far as executing your dreams and visions are concerned. However, once they begin to see your achievements, they would like to come and join you. This is an interesting dynamic and almost every Pastor or anyone in leadership roles has those kind of people around them. They will doubt you from the beginning, but immediately as they begin to see your accomplishments and fruits of your vision or goal, they will be quick to tell you how they always believed in you and how, although they were not very visible, they were praying for you in their closet. If you have ever served in any leadership role or capacity and you've never met any such persons in your life, then perhaps you are just fortunate.

As a Pastor and one who has taken many leadership roles in various initiatives and under various circumstances, both on my regular job and in the work of the ministry, I have met quite a number of people who exhibit the "Thomas dynamics" described above. Even in the Church, one would find such people from time to time.

My most recent memory of having to deal with the behavior pattern of such people was during the purchasing of our Church property. Although every detail of the sales transaction for the property was made known to all our key members and I took the time to explain to them the reason why going after the property would be very beneficial to the ministry at large and to the general growth of our Church. Not all were strongly on-board with the idea of purchasing the property. Although the "*Thomases*" seemed not to voice their objections to the idea of purchasing the property, neither were they for it because as you would normally find them, they were on the sidelines waiting to see which side seemed to be winning.

As usual and as one would expect them to behave, they stood on the sidelines and watch to see if anything positive would come out of the Church's effort to raise the funds needed within the short period of time we had at hand to purchase the property. Although they knew it was a good thing if we could acquire the property, they, at the same time, were hesitant to contribute towards the fund-raising effort, just in case it failed and we were unable to recover the money invested in the sales deal. It was not until I had worked closely with those members who strongly believed and supported the vision and idea to purchase the building that the "Thomases" who were on the sidelines decided to join in.

Remember I mentioned earlier that even with the "*Thomases*" you may have in your life, be careful you do not cast them away, because you might need them later when circumstances are more conducive. It is interesting to note what happened next after we acquired the building. We needed funds to renovate portions of the interior of the building, in addition to purchasing about 150 chairs, and guess who was chief among those that were instrumental in getting this portion accomplished? It was the *"Thomases."* Some of the same people who doubted the Church's ability to close on the deal to purchase the building now joined in the effort to renovate and furnish it. If I remember quite well, some of these initial doubters contributed well towards the interior renovation and furnishing of the church building. Be careful not to run the *"Thomases"* out because their contribution will be needed at an opportune time.

> **Having people like the "Thomases" around you sometimes fuels and propels your ambition and eventually leads you to successfully accomplish things that you never thought you would be able to accomplish.**

The *"Thomases"* would stand afar off and watch your progress until they were convinced that something positive was going to come out of your effort, and then they would come to join you. Once they are convinced and with you, they contribute their best to the agenda.

THE ZEALOTS (Simon the Zealot).

Simon the Zealot's name was not mentioned much in the gospel accounts, but this is the man who came to Jesus with his own agenda at hand. Like Simon the Zealot did in his association with Jesus, some may join themselves to you, not so much because of your agenda, but rather because you have an agenda that will further their agenda. That was a man by name of Simon the Zealot. He joined himself to Jesus, not because of Jesus' Kingdom business, but rather for the sake of the political freedom of Israel. At the time of Jesus, Israel was a nation under Roman rule and governance, and as his name strongly suggests, the Zealots were die-hard political activists who at the time were causing riots, insurrection and unrest among the Jewish people in order to revolt against and over throw the Roman government.

They were partisan for Jewish political independence and to such a group did Simon the Zealot belong. It is no secret that Jesus might have been aware of Simon the Zealot's political agenda, yet he selected him to be part of the 12 disciples. Isn't that interesting? The reason why Jesus might have overlooked Simon the Zealot's political interest or agenda is because people like that would later come to see your commitment to them, and your commitment to them would change the dynamics of the relationship you had with them.

Now watch how the five dynamics of friendship mentioned earlier in the chapter played out in the life of the disciples who were with Jesus. According to Jesus, in **Mark 3:14,** he called the 12 disciples so they would be with him. ***"And he ordained twelve, that they should be with him, and that He might send them forth to preach."***

Even more than that, Jesus called his disciples so they would ***comfort, cover, carry, caution*** and finally show ***care*** for one another. This is what I referred to earlier in this chapter as the 5 C's of a true and genuine friendship or relationship. The 5 C's of a true and genuine friendship or relationship would help you to identify whether who you call friends and whether they are indeed true and genuine or not.

1. True Relationships bring Comfort.

A Friend will *comfort* you, and so your friends are supposed to be your source of comfort. Much of the comfort of this life lies in friendship that comes with prudence and which are virtuous. Your friends are supposed to be in your life to *comfort* you, and you to comfort them. The friends of Job came purposely to comfort him in his calamities, and as mentioned briefly and in one of the previous chapters, it is very interesting how the three friends of Job go about comforting him. Job 2:11-13 says that they purposely arranged to meet him in order to provide comfort. What is surprising in this case however, is the way they went about it. It was not as one would usually expect to see. Upon seeing first-hand how grave Job's sorrow was, they sat together with him for seven days and seven nights without uttering a word.

> **Job 2:11-13** *"Now when Job's three friends heard of all this evil that was come upon him, they came everyone from his own place, Eliphaz the Temanite, and Bildad the Shuhite, and Zophar the Naamathite: for they had made an appointment together to come to mourn with him and to* **comfort him.** *[12] And when they lifted up their eyes afar off, and knew him not, they lifted up their voice, and wept, and they rent everyone his mantle, and sprinkled dust upon their heads toward heaven. [13] So they sat down with him upon the ground seven days and seven nights, and none spake a word unto him: for they saw that his grief was very great."*

They did not say a word to him, nor to each other but sat in the situation with him. Job had ashes upon his head and so did they put ashes on their head. Job rented his clothes and so did they. Job sat on the ground and so did they.

True Friendship is an amazing thing because true friends will embrace you in whatever you are going through and will be willing to join you even without understanding the cause of your predicament.

As mentioned earlier, there are certain situations in life that one goes through where "words" in themselves are insufficient to express comfort towards the one going through the situation. In those circumstances, what you need is not people who will come around and try to make up words, but rather, people who are willing to just come and sit with you in your affliction or trouble. This is because in most cases when people say they understand your situation because they have experienced something similar, they still don't really understand.

Every situation of grief and sorrow is unique, one from the other. It's a hard thing to say, but mourning the passing away or separation from an abusive husband or wife is not the same as mourning the passing away or separation of a loving and extremely caring husband or wife. Some people don't really care when their husband or wife is separated from them in any way or by any means because their presence in their lives caused them more pain and grief than being pleasant, a blessing or comfort.

In my studies and research toward the writing of this book, I found out that the word "companion" in most occasions in the Bible, is used to describe the "sharing of the unpleasant side of friendship." Let me break this statement down for your understanding:

As an example, consider the following Bible passages and examine what each of them is pointing to about "companionship."

Rev. 1:19. *Companion in tribulation*

Philp 2:25 *Companion in labor*

Hebrew10:33 *Companion in suffering*

Acts 19:25 *Companion in chaos*

(In reference to Ephesus, the city of goddess Diana where there was an uproar among the people to persecute Paul and his companions.)

The lesson this is teaching us about the word companion is that, companionship would not always be under pleasant circumstances.

There may be times in your life when you would need friends who will mourn with you or you with them in their moments of grief. That is why the Bible admonishes the believer to mourn with them that mourn and sorrow with them that sorrow.

2. True Relationships bring Covering.

Your true friends are supposed to be your covering blanket, the kind of friends that even when you do something wrong, would not expose you but rather correct you. A friend that will cover you even when you are in a mess of a situation or find yourself in some unpleasant circumstances. There are some who may argue that, the covering of someone means you are partaking in their sins, and they will quote Bible verses like, "Be ye not a partaker of another man's sins." However, that does not necessarily apply in all situations, because love has a way of covering a multitude of sins according to the Bible.

Some also will, under the pretense of self-righteousness, expose others in order to make themselves appear to be more righteous. But the devil is always a liar because *a true friend will cover you.* They will not cover you in order to encourage the occurrence of your faults or sins but rather, cover you in order to help restore you.

There is a difference between exposing someone and covering them when they fall to sin. What one has to realize is that exposure is a greater condemnation than coverage.

Galatians 6:1 therefore teaches us that:

"Brethren, if a man be overtaken in a fault, ye which are spiritual, restore such a one in the spirit of meekness; considering thyself, lest thou also be tempted."

The Bible says in *II Corinthians 5:18* that God has given us the ministry of reconciliation. Therefore, as Christians, we are called unto restoration and not exposure and condemnation.

True friends are supposed to be your safety blanket. They will cover you to protect you even when you are already at fault, in order to shield you from further hurt and harm. The way we handle others in their faults can either heal and restore them or drive them even into the extremes of the very conditions they have fallen to. Hence, they will be more tactical, merciful and compassionate the next time a brother or sister falls to sin.

3. True Friends Will Carry you.

True friends are in your life to carry you across hard life terrains and circumstances. They are supposed to be your clutches to help you stand on your feet and your harness to prevent you from further falls in life. God forbid, but if you are to lose your strength or your ability to carry on the burdens of life, true friends will help you carry on.

There is a remarkable story in the gospel of **Mark 2:3** that tells of how four men carried their friend who was sick of palsy unto the roof of a house where Jesus was lodging. Jesus was surrounded by so great a crowd of people that they were unable to penetrate and get close to him. When they realized that they couldn't carry their friend on a bed into the house where Jesus was because of the crowd, they tore up the roof over the house Jesus was lodging in and bored a hole in the ceiling so they could carry their friend into the presence of Jesus.

This is a remarkable story because it shows how far true and genuine friends would go to see their friend who is suffering have relief from his condition. Think about this carefully. For a moment, they cared less about who owned the building. They cared less about how dangerous it was to climb unto a roof of a house with their bed-ridden friend who was on a stretcher. They cared less about the fact that they were damaging the roof of some homeowner, for the sake of their friend's healing and deliverance. They cared less about the fact that they may have to come up with money to repair the roof regardless of whether their friend got healed or not.

This means they whole-heartedly accepted responsibility for damaging someone's roof. It means they also accepted the cost of repairing the roof irrespective of whether their friend received healing or not. Their primary and only aim at the moment was to lighten the burden of their friend who was suffering from palsy. All other considerations were secondary at the time. This brings me back to the point I made earlier in this chapter, and that is, exposing people in their faults is a greater condemnation than covering them.

You cannot lift people up in their low estate and help them stand back on their feet, if you are in the business of exposing people.

That will just not work because the two (exposure and covering) are opposite and contrary one to the other. In conclusion to this segment of the chapter, are you in the business of exposing your brothers and sisters when they fall to sin or covering them in order to aid in their healing and restoration? You judge for yourself.

4. True Relationships bring Care.

Allow me to introduce you to the care of a true friend through a passage of Scripture recorded in **Luke 11:5-8 (KJV)**:

"And he said unto them, which of you shall have a friend, and shall go unto him at midnight, and say unto him, Friend, lend me three loaves, [6] For a friend of mine in his journey is come to me, and I have nothing to set before him? [7] And he from within shall answer and say, trouble me not: the door is now shut, and my children are with me in bed; I cannot rise and give thee. [8] I say unto you, though he will not rise and give him, because he is his friend, yet because of his importunity he will rise and give him as many as he needeth."

Notice what the 8th verse says. Although it was an inconvenience to be knocking at his friend's door in the middle of the night, yet because he was a friend, he overlooked all the inconvenience and showed care to the friend. That is what true friends do for one another. They come to one another's aid even when circumstances are not conducive.

> **If you have friends who go "missing in action" during your moments of grief or in your down seasons in life, I strongly advise you to reconsider your association with them.**

Perhaps what you may need to do is to trim them off from your sphere or circle of friends because they don't deserve to be called your friend. Jesus no doubt used this story to teach us about the degree to which our heavenly Father cares about us, although at times our actions may not be what He expects of us.

5. True Friends Will Caution you

True friends are supposed to be your Godly Positioning System (GPS) to you. Their counsel and words of caution are supposed to guard, guide and position you onto a godly path.

True friends will see danger ahead and they will warn or caution you. This is a very important quality of a true friend because caution will save you from a lot of headaches and troubles. The Bible says in **Proverbs 24:6** that *"in the multitude of counsellors, there is safety."* So, here again, a true friend becomes your safety blanket to protect you from troubles that lie ahead.

There is a remarkable story in the Bible about the friendship between David and Jonathan. If Saul was the King of Israel, then it obviously means that his son Jonathan would be the crown Prince, the one who was next in line to the throne of Israel. However, when Jonathan heard that Saul, his father, was planning to kill his friend David who had become a very good friend to Jonathan, he began to caution David in order to protect and save David's life from the evil and wicked ambitions of his father.

It could have been that King Saul was probably planning to kill David to preserve the throne for his son, Jonathan. One cannot under-estimate what parents will do for their children until the defining moments are at hand. We are not very sure if that was the case with King Saul, but it is totally possible that his goal in desiring the death of David was to preserve the throne for his son, Jonathan. On the other hand, his son, Jonathan, was least concerned about ascending to the throne of his father, knowing that God had already ordained his friend David to succeed his father.

I wonder what you would have done if you were to find yourself in the place of Jonathan, knowing that the friend you are trying to save is the one who is destined to take your throne. Perhaps, because of the strong friendship and bond between the two, Jonathan was at peace with the fact that God had chosen his friend David to be King after his father left the throne. Although ascending to the throne of Israel was the right of Jonathan by birth, he yielded to the will of God and instead, protected his friend David. What do you do when you are next in line for a position and someone who happened to be your best friend is put there in that position instead of you? None of these plans, however, seemed to bother Jonathan more than his loyalty to his friend, David.

Jonathan went and cautioned David that his father Saul was planning to kill him in a bid to protect him from his father. Even to the extent that Jonathan stripped himself of what would most likely be his robe and put them on David to disguise and protect him from any harm from his father. The Bible says that on that day David made a covenant with Jonathan. Jonathan said to David, "I will protect you from my father until you ascend to the throne of my father." In other words, what Jonathan was saying to David was that, "I will forfeit my position as next on the throne and give to you what rightfully belongs to me by birthright because God has ordained you to ascend to the throne."

As Jonathan died in war when he was killed together with his father, King Saul, in the hills of Gilboa by the sword of the Philistines, David mourned his friend Jonathan. In honor of Jonathan, he wrote a special song in tribute to Saul and Jonathan which became known as the song of the Bow. The words of this song can be found in the book of Jasher which is by interpretation, the book of the upright as recorded in **2 Samuel 1:17-21.**

> *"And David lamented with this lamentation over Saul and over Jonathan his son: [18] (Also he bade them teach the children of Judah the use of the bow: behold, it is written in the book of Jasher. [book of the Upright]) [19] The beauty of Israel is slain upon thy high places: how are the mighty fallen! [20] Tell it not in Gath, publish it not in the streets of Askelon; lest the daughters of the Philistines rejoice, lest the daughters of the uncircumcised triumph. [21] Ye mountains of Gilboa, let there be no dew, neither let there be rain, upon you, nor fields of offerings: for there the shield of the mighty is vilely cast away, the shield of Saul, as though he had not been anointed with oil."*

Do you have friends like David or like Jonathan in your life? It's about time you get out of this secular garbage that new age technology has termed social media and be connected to the godly men and women that God has assigned to your life, to impact your life for the good. Oh, it will make so much sense to you when they show up in your life.

In closing this chapter, when you take a critical look at the 5 dynamics of friendship, you should realize that friends are human extensions of the Holy Spirit. That's why, as a Spirit-filled Believer, it's going to be very difficult for you to walk with people who don't believe what you believe because true friends in our lives are supposed to be living examples of the Holy Spirit. Their touch is supposed to be as the touch of God. Their counsel is supposed to be to you the counsel of God. Their comfort is supposed to be to you, as the comfort of God and finally, their covering is supposed to be same as God's covering.

'Food-For-Thought'
Worksheet for Chapter 5

The S.W.A.G Test. (Continued)

*Are the People you call Friends, **SMART, WISE, AMICABLE & GODLY**?*

1. In addition to the S.W.A.G. Test, do the people I call friends, companions or confidants possess the qualities that makes up what is termed in Chapter 5 of this book the **5 Cs of Friendship?**

2. As a litmus test about whether or not you have the **5 Cs of friendship, carefully examine if the person(s) you call** friends, companions or confidants are the type who would bring into your life the following:

   Comfort—True friends will COMFORT you in order to ease your pain.

   Covering—True Friends will COVER you from harm or further destruction.

   Carriage—True friends will CARRY you by providing a support system.

   Care—True friends will show CARE for you when you cannot help yourself.

   Caution—True friends will CAUTION you when they sense trouble or danger ahead. They will be your GPS (Godly Positioning System).

3. If the friends you have don't meet these 5 Cs of friendship criteria above, re-consider admitting such person(s) into your inner sphere of friendship, or else you will have yourself and yourself alone to blame.

4. Word of Caution: Friends with these qualities serve as extensions of the Holy Spirit in the life of the Believer, so hold them dearly to yourself when you come across such friends in your life. In case friends with such qualities are totally absent from your life, diligently ask God to allow such friends to cross your path.

CHAPTER 6

FRIENDS, IT IS YOUR CHOICE, NOT THEIR'S.

> To reach your God-given potential and realize the full capacity of what God has put in you, you cannot walk along with just any and everybody

NOTICE THAT FROM the main text for this subject and as recorded in Luke 6, where we find Jesus' model of relationships, he prayed for God's guidance in order to choose his disciples. Also, one thing that is worth noting about the text is that they don't select him, he selects them. At times you have people upset with you simply because they want to be your friend or be around you, and somehow, they feel you are not responding positively enough to them. Some, get upset and offended as if they are entitled to be your friend or as if your life is their domain. Isn't that something scary?

There is a beautiful piece of Scripture in John 15:16 which directly addresses this subject, and which is like a nail on the head of the subject of choosing your friends and sphere of relationships. In this text, Jesus said plainly to his disciples that, *[16] "Ye have not chosen me, but I have chosen you, and ordained you, that ye should go and bring forth fruit, and that your fruit should remain: that whatsoever ye shall ask of the Father in my name, he may give it you."*

Do not let yourself go into any kind or form of relationship because you feel a morbid obligation or pressure to do so or else you will have none but yourself to blame down the line.

In the verse that precedes, (John 15:15), Jesus elevated the status of his disciples to friends when he said to them, *[15] "Henceforth I call you not servants, for the servant knoweth not what his lord doeth: but I have called you friends, for all things that I have heard of my Father I have made known unto you."*

At times you may wonder why some people clamor around you when they notice that you are not responding positively to their advances to be your friend. Think through carefully who you would like to be close to, as well as pray for God's guidance in your choice as Jesus did. Even after you have chosen your friends, you still have to watch their character and the motions around you to ensure that, like Jesus, you don't choose any "devil" among your circle of friends. If it happened to Jesus, it could also happen to you, so be on your guard. The reason for caution and vigilance in choosing who your friends should be is this:

> **Although we all walk one foot after the other, we do not necessarily take the same steps or walk the same paths in life.**

Although we meet at Church together, have fellowship and worship together, our destinies are not tied one to another. Your calling is different from mine and so is my calling different from yours or that of the other person you relate to.

Friends—You Choose Them.

Jesus went on to say, *"You have not chosen me, but I have chosen you that ye may be fruitful."* So again, the purpose of relationships is so you would be fruitful.

> **If you find yourself in a relationship or association of any kind, be it spiritual, social, educational or business, that is not making you fruitful, then it is about time you give it up and get out of it.**

In choosing you circles of friendship, you need to do it wisely, and I mean very wisely, because unhealthy relationships always come with a dear price to pay.

The following are some simple but helpful guidelines for you to follow when choosing your friends:

1. **Make sure you choose them, and not that they choose you.** If *folks are going to be upset because they are not going to be close to you, that is their business; let them deal with it, but you make sure you choose them.*

2. **Choose them carefully.** At times we push our way to be close to people, only to find out that they are not who we thought they were. Should that happen to you, don't be a victim or a prisoner of your own choice. Simply find a way to move on so you don't become a victim.

3. **Choose them prayerfully.** Don't allow anyone to just show up overnight in your life or in your sphere of influence. Watch while you pray, and pray while you watch. Watch their motions (motives), watch their character and watch who their other friends are and that will give you a clue to know whether they are the right friends for you or not.

4. Have you ever observed someone from afar off and admired them, but gotten closer only to find out that this definitely might be a mistake on your part to want to be with them? I have, and I must confess that it was a great lesson for me. However, I did not allow myself to be a victim of my choice. I pulled myself away gradually until I had no connection with this person. You have to be careful in choosing

because I have found that one can get an impartation even without having to be too close to one another. Relationships and associations definitely have a way of either positively or negatively impacting our lives.

5. **As you make your selection, be mindful of the number and limit it to just what you have the capacity to handle.**

Notice that the closer the companionship Jesus desired, the lesser the number he chose. He started with the crowds that followed Him, but He did not end up with the crowds at the point of His death. His relationship sphere went down from the multitudes, to the 70 disciples whom He sent out in pairs, to the 12 He chose to be closer to Him, and finally to the 3 inner core and confidants, namely Peter, James and John.

So, you see by now how "crazy" it is when people boast about having 100s, 1000s, and millions of followers on Facebook and Twitter. Either you're wasting their time or they're wasting your time. The numbers should and must go down if you truly seek closeness in relationships. That's just how we were made to function, so the earlier we learn it from the life of Jesus, the better and the more effective we will be in all our human relationships.

Don't be afraid to trim down your friendship wardrobe and to cut down the number and limit them graciously. You don't have the capacity to handle too much around you, because a true relationship requires a withdrawal from you. How much can you give out without running empty? How much can you handle without running dry? How much can you communicate with without being distracted?

There are people who have run dry of their relationship capital because they have spent all their relational capital or energy on strangers they met on social media or around people who didn't have their well-being at heart. So, what happens in such a relationship is that they keep giving until they have nothing left to give. You cannot be constantly giving out without finding a way to replenish your energy. After you have given your best, you also need someone who can pour into you the virtue that has gone out.

> **After you have fed and poured into others, what you need is someone who will also feed you and pour into you in order for you to regain your spiritual stamina.**

If you don't have such a person in your circle of relationship, you will definitely run dry and burn out both physically and spiritually.

> **Many Pastors do a good job in feeding the flock over which they are shepherds. However, they fail to find a means of feeding their spiritual man, so their strength will be rejuvenated after virtue is gone out of them.**

This is especially true for Pastors. Spiritual burned-out is one of the most common crises that people in a pastoral role go through. The very reason why so many people in ministry get burn-out, especially Pastors, is because some Pastors do a good job in feeding the flock that they are shepherds over. However, they fail to find a means of feeding their spiritual man, so their strength will be rejuvenated after virtue is gone out of them.

When the woman with the blood issue touched Jesus, do you remember what Jesus said? He said, virtue is gone out of me because somebody touched me. So, as Pastors and Ministers, as we touch lives by doing the work of the ministry, our lives must also be touched and replenished spiritually and even physically as well because none of us is super-human. We all go dry on our spiritual strength and stamina from time to time.

When people become burned out and lack the energy and virtue to continue, they develop the tendency to freak out when any little thing goes wrong in their relationship.

True relationships are covenantal. Covenants, by their nature, define our relationship one to another. Therefore, before you go into another relationship, ask yourself a few questions like:

1. What are you bringing to the relationship?

2. What do you wish to get out of this relationship that will make you a better person than you were before?

3. What are your expectations and that of the other person?

4. Are those expectations realistic or just a fantasy?

By so doing, you will find out that there are a couple of people who are just hanging around you for nothing and with whom you would not like any level of closeness. They're not making you any better, so it's a waste of each person's time. Although work has defined boundaries, when it comes to relationship, many people don't want to engage in it within defined boundaries because they do not see the importance of it. Where there are no well-defined boundaries, there are unfulfilled expectations. This is so because many people don't take the time to assess their relationships.

Our basic humanitarian needs include the need to be loved and touched. That's just how we were made. Consider this, do you realize that human beings were the only creation of God that God had to touch in the process of creating? It's like telling the fish to take swimming lessons. If only they could speak they would definitely tell you that they don't need lessons because swimming is what they were created to do anyway. The paradox however is that, because swimming is what they were created to do, that's the very reason why they may need to take swimming lessons in order to better their skills in swimming. When you make the extra effort towards being critical in choosing your friends it will definitely not hurt or harm but can only help. So why don't you put some effort into your relationships with others?

'Food-For-Thought'
Worksheet for Chapter 6

1. **Make sure you choose your friends. Do not let them choose you.**

2. **In the process of choosing your friends, choose them carefully and wisely.**

3. **Choose them prayerfully:** Do not allow anyone to just show up in your life or in your sphere of influence overnight.

4. **What should I watch out for when choosing my friends?**
   - Watch their motions,
   - Watch their motives
   - Watch their character
   - Watch who their other friends are and that will give you a clue about who they are.

5. **As you make your selection, be mindful of the number and limit it to just what you have the capacity to handle.**

6. Should you realize that you have made the wrong choice, what do you do?

- Don't panic and don't be rude. It's not the end of the world.

- Don't feel in any way obligated to stick to it. Rather, retrace the steps that led you into that friendship and make a diligent effort to pull yourself away gradually and tactfully.

CHAPTER 7

MOVING BEYOND YOUR PAST, STEPPING INTO YOUR DESTINY

MANY PEOPLE LIVE their lives in bitterness and resentment from past relationships that did not end well. Your encounter with destiny would not come until you have been able to move on beyond your past in order to step into your God-given destiny. One thing every one of us needs to watch and not become a victim of is our past. Most often in life, discouragements come not from the unknown or the things that we have never encountered before. Discouragement usually comes from the bad memories of our experiences.

Living your past in your present can be a hindrance to your future.

In the book of Numbers, the Bible talks about a man by the name of Hobab. ***"29. Moses said unto Hobab, the son of Raguel the Midianite, Moses' father-in-law, we are journeying unto the place of which the Lord said, I will give it you: come thou with us, and we will do thee good: for the Lord hath spoken good concerning Israel. [30] And he said unto him, I will not go; but I will depart to mine own land, and to my kindred. [31] And he said, Leave us not, I pray thee, forasmuch as thou knowest how we are to encamp in the wilderness, and thou mayest be to us instead of eyes. [32] And it shall be, if thou go with us, yea, it shall be, that what goodness the Lord shall do unto us, the same will we do unto thee. [33] And they departed from the mount of the Lord three days' journey: and the ark of the covenant of the Lord went before them in the three days' journey, to search out a resting place for them."*** (**Numbers 10:29-33**)

Hobab, we know from Scripture, was a man of black descent. But what we are not sure about is whether he was the son of Jethro (Moses' father-in-law) or Jethro himself. Either way, that does not change his descent because Jethro we know, was a Medianite Priest and Media was the son of Abraham through a woman by the name of Keturah because after the death of Sarah, Abraham took Keturah as wife and had 6 sons with Keturah.

When the Israelites who were supposed to be the people with the vision left Egypt and did not know their way through the desert, Moses, invited Hobab to lead them through the desert and to show them the way, because Hobab knew the in-roads through the wilderness terrain. Hobab refused to go with them. That was a missed opportunity because you don't necessarily have to be the one with the vision, but you can share in the leader's vision.

I want to show you how important this was, and the magnitude of the opportunity missed by Hobab. In verse 31, we are told that Moses pleaded with Hobab to be the eyes of a young nation that God was about to raise to fame and power. *[31] And he said, leave us not, I pray thee, for as much as thou knowest how we are to encamp in the wilderness, and thou mayest be to us instead of eyes."* That was a voice of desperation and frustration, because Moses did not have a clue as to how to journey safely into Canaan.

On top of that, Moses made a promise to Hobab and said, *"We will likewise bless you when the Lord blesses us, so please, come with us and be to us an eye through the wilderness."* That is like giving Hobab a rain check of a blessing because at the time Israel had not yet been blessed by the Lord. But they were certain that the hand of God was upon them and hence they would be blessed. Hobab, however, missed this blessing of the Almighty God because:

You can share in other people's blessing only when you have shared in their vision.

Therefore, what you need to do is to line yourself up with the person with the vision, but Hobab refused to do that. This leads me to my main point and that is, Hobab, found himself in the midst of something extremely great, and the sad thing is that he did not even recognize the essence of that moment. Let me tell you, friend, we must be watchful because:

....

You can be in the midst of a great window of opportunity that perhaps could be the best thing that will ever happen to you and not know it.

....

That's what happened to Hobab and as a result he missed what would have been his moment with God. *Hence you would notice that from that moment on, no mention was made of Hobab in the pages of Scripture.*

He was invited to be the eye of a nation and he ignorantly, selfishly, or for whatever reason, turned his back on the window of opportunity. Just be careful you don't miss your kairos (critical) moment with God, because it is God who arranges for us to meet people who impact our lives. It is God who arranges circumstances, opportunities and encounters in our lives. He literally pulls some people into our lives so they will impact our lives and at times pushes others out so we will be able to reach our destiny. For many people, because of indifference, or feeling of intimidation, or for whatever reasons, they fail to recognize these theophoric (God-centered) encounters with God in our lives.

I don't know how far I would have gone especially in the work of the ministry if God had not brought some people into my life and ministry. At times, I wonder how things would have been if some of the strides I have made in life by God's grace were absent from my life. Jacob, certainly did not miss his moment with God because after a wrestling match with the angel of the Lord all night, he said to the angel, you must be someone special so bless me before you leave. How many people, after being defeated in a wrestling match, would ask their winning opponent for a blessing?

Hobab, was short-sighted in that he saw in Moses and the Jews the *weakness* of a contingent of slaves coming out of Egypt. What he failed to see was the hand of the Almighty God who was with Israel. He failed to see the might of the *All-sufficient God* who was leading Israel. Therefore, coming back to the point I made earlier in this chapter,

You can be in the midst of something pivotal and momentous and not know it because you are focusing on the trivial.

If you doubt this statement, let me prove it to you from the 22nd chapter of Luke's gospel.

15] And he said unto them, with desire I have desired to eat this Passover with you before I suffer: [16] For I say unto you, I will not any more eat thereof, until it be fulfilled in the kingdom of God. [17] And he took the cup, and gave thanks, and said, Take this, and divide it among yourselves. [19] And he took bread, and gave thanks, and brake it, and gave unto them, saying, this is my body which is given for you: this do in remembrance of me. [20] Likewise also the cup after supper, saying, this cup is the new testament in my blood, which is shed for you. [21] But, behold, the hand of him that betrayeth me is with me on the table. [23] And they began to enquire among themselves, which of them it was that should do this thing. [24] And there was also a strife among them, which of them should be accounted the greatest.

"And the Lord said, Simon, Simon, behold, Satan hath desired to have you, that he may sift you as wheat: [32] But I have prayed for thee that thy faith fails not: and when thou art converted (turned around) strengthen thy brethren. (make thy brotherhood strong) [33] And he said unto him, Lord, I am ready to go with thee, both into prison, and to death. [34] And he said, I tell thee, Peter, the cock shall not crow this day, before that thou shalt thrice deny that thou knowest me."

(Luke 22:31-34)

The time of this text is interesting because it occurred during the last few hours before Jesus was betrayed by Judas, taken away by the Jews, and crucified by the Roman Soldiers. The ministry of Jesus for all its intent and purposes was about drawing to an end and in order to fulfill the specific purpose for which He was brought into this world. He saw the need to prepare Himself towards His ultimate end, which was the death on the cross. It seems like He was right on schedule because His death was imminent, and all roads were about to lead to the place of His final moment on earth.

The time of the text was at the communion table, popularly known as the Last Supper in the upper room, and it was at this occasion that Jesus was about to institute something new. He was about to institute what would become one of the most sacred ordinances of the Church. What would later become known as the Holy Communion.

At the communion table on this very important occasion, it is interesting to note that a number of things were going on: It was a time of great fellowship, and that we obviously know. However, what we don't often notice about that fateful night around the dinner table was that it was also a time of great conflict. I would like to draw your attention to at least three things that were going on at the table.

1. Jesus said, the person who is going to betray me is sitting at the table with me (**Verse 21**).

2. The disciples, we are told, also began to question each other about who it was that was going to do such a terrible thing (**Verse 23**).

3. The context also tells us that there was something else going on according to Verse 24, which was very important to note as well. There was the spirit of competition and strife among His disciples about which of them should be counted the greatest among them (**Verse 24**).

All these were going on at the communion table. You know you can be in the midst of something great and critical going on and you don't even know it. You can be in the midst of something *pivotal,* and instead of focusing your attention on it, you can be caught up in focusing on the trivial things that have very little or no value.

HERE IT IS—the greatest thing ever to happen in human history was about to take place and the people who happened to be chosen to witness it and to tell the rest of humanity, although they were present at the table, were focusing on the trivial.

HERE IT IS—what would become one of the key ordinances of the New Testament Church was about to be instituted by Christ and the people who were honored to be present at the table were otherwise minded.

HERE IT IS—at the verge of history making, the disciples were not paying attention to the significance of the moment because from that night onward history was about to be split in two. Meaning, henceforth, time would be known as Before Christ (BC) and After Death of Christ (AD).

So, this death of Jesus, which was imminent and was about to happen, was the purpose for which he was born and the purpose for which these 12 disciples present at the table were selected to be witnesses. Yet judging from what their focus was at the table, it was obvious that they had no clue how critical the moment they were about to witness was. Rather, they were fighting among themselves about who was going to be the greatest, which by the way was not important because Jesus had already taught them that he who wants to be the greatest must be the servant.

Also, at the Mt. of Transfiguration, here we are told that the three disciples (Peter, James and John) that Jesus specifically handpicked to observe this crucial event, and to tell the rest of the world, went to sleep. For that reason, today, we have no manuscript of whatever conversation transpired between Jesus, Moses and Elijah. Today, all we have about that event are speculations about the conversation that really transpired.

Luke 19: 43-44. *"For the days (chronos) shall come upon thee, that thine enemies shall cast a trench about thee, and compass thee round, and keep thee in on every side, [44] And shall lay thee even with the ground, and thy children within thee, and they shall not leave in thee one stone upon another, because thou knowest not the time (kairos- appointed time) of thy visitation."* Meaning, our encounter with God could come but it's possible you could miss it.

> **The greatest enemy of your future is when you allow the failures or successes of your past to stand in the way.**

Leaving Your Past Behind.

One of the major elements that hinders your moment with God and which you need to watch lest you wither and die, is your past. A fellow once said, *"What stands between our present and our future prospects is our past."* Therefore:

Thus, your past is something that you need to guard against, so you don't faint and die before the promises of God are fulfilled in your life. Every one of us has a past. When you are in your moment of encounter with God, it's important that you do not bring your relative past into that moment.

Learning To Let Go

The spider monkey is a tiny animal native to South and Central America. Quick as lightning, it's a very difficult animal to capture in the wild. For years, people attempted to shoot spider monkeys with tranquilizer guns or capture them with nets, but they discovered that the spider monkeys were nearly always faster than their fastest draw or quickest trap. Then somebody discovered the best method for capturing this elusive creature was to take a clear, narrow-mouthed glass bottle, put one peanut inside it, and wait. The spider monkey then reaches into the bottle to get the peanut and it won't get its hand out of the bottle as long as it is clenching the peanut. The bottle is so heavy compared to its weight, so it can't drag the bottle with it. The spider monkey is too persistent to let go of a peanut once it has grasped it. It is said that in fact a wheelbarrow full of peanuts or bananas can be dumped right next to the spider monkey, and it won't let go of that one peanut.

How many of us are like that? Unwilling to change a habit? Be a little flexible or give up something we know is bringing destruction to our lives. We stubbornly cling to things and people even if it brings pain and suffering. Don't cling to a negative situation that may drain your vitality and energy. Learn to let go and let God have his way in your life.

You may never lose your taste for peanuts by letting them go at times, but with the Lord's help, you can discern when peanuts are traps in glass bottles.

(Taken from "Quiet moments with God, Devotional: 6th Edition" page 84-85, prepared by W.B. Freeman Concepts Inc., Tulsa-OK)

Philippians 3:13-14 *forgetting those things which are behind, and reaching forth unto those things which are before, I press towards the mark for the prize of the high calling of GOD in Christ Jesus.*

I am going to prove to you from the eleventh chapter of the book of Genesis how holding on to your relative past can be a hindrance to your future.

> *"29] And Abram and Nahor took them wives: the name of Abram's wife was Sarai; and the name of Nahor's wife, Milcah, the daughter of Haran, the father of Milcah, and the father of Iscah. [30] But Sarai was barren; she had no child. [31] And* **Terah took Abram** *his son, and Lot the son of Haran his son's son, and Sarai his daughter-in-law, his son Abram's wife,* **and they went forth with them** *from Ur of the Chaldees, to go into the land of Canaan, and they came unto Haran, and dwelt there."* **(Genesis 11:29-31)**

From the above passage of Scripture, I would like you to notice that it was Terah, the father of Abraham, who was taking Abraham along and not the other way around. There is a big problem about this because God spoke to Abraham and not Terah. The text says "And *Terah took* Abraham his son." But wait a minute, where was *Terah* taking Abraham and the others? Also, why was it *Terah* who was taking Abraham when, as a matter of fact, God appeared unto Abraham and not Terah and God gave Abraham the promise, not Terah?

The passage goes on to say, **"and they went forth with them."** Therefore, the big question one ought to ask is, *who are the* **"They"** *and who are* **"Them?"**

Why is it Terah taking Abraham to Canaan in the first place? The "*they*" refers to Abraham and Sarah and the "*them*" refers to Terah the father of Abraham, Lot the nephew of Abraham, their servants and all other folks who should not be going on this journey, but are nevertheless on the journey with Abraham and Sarah.

A reference and confirmation to this passage can be found in the following passage of Scripture, ***"The God of glory appeared unto our father Abraham, when he was in Mesopotamia, before he dwelt in Charran, [3] And said unto him, Get thee out of thy country, and from thy kindred, and come into the land which I shall shew thee."*** (Acts 7:2-3)

The passage above confirms the fact that God appeared unto Abraham and not his father Terah, and the instructions that God gave to Abraham were very clear. He was supposed to come out from among his family to be led by God unto a land that God had promised to give to him and his descendants. So, Terah was not supposed to be on this journey, and Lot was also not supposed to go on this journey either, and so are all the other folks who were with them. So, when you refer to Genesis 12:1 it begins with the phrase, ***"and now the Lord had said to Abraham."*** That's in the past tense, meaning that the Lord first spoke to Abram (Abraham), before Terah decided to take them and so God had to wait on Abraham to sort himself out from his past before bringing him into his future.

If you are ever going to move into dominion with God or ascend to higher heights and greater levels of closeness to God, it requires that you leave behind your "relative" past.

Your relative past are the things that you are close to, and have intimate closeness to. This includes your old mindset and the people that cannot go with you into your future but you are still close to them. Even some stuff that you deem important

that you may want to bring along with you, God says no—
You can't carry those things with you if you wish to have an
encounter with Me.

So, God had to wait on Abraham. God had to wait for Terah
to die out of Abraham's life before God reappeared again to
talk with Abraham, because Terah was not supposed to be on
the journey to start with. The implication here is that for many
people, there is no shadow of doubt that God has called them
into something great or into a special relationship or destiny.
However, what is delaying their breakthrough is the stuff that
they are hanging on to from their past. I will also prove to you
later that Lot was also not supposed to be on this journey and as
a result, his presence caused Abraham a lot of headache along
the journey.

What God was saying to Abraham from the very beginning
when He gave him the word of promise was that, "I just want
you and Sarah to go to Canaan and no one else." Therefore, the
reason why Sarah was still barren and could not have the son
of promise was because if she couldn't have that child in the
land of the Chaldees, then she must have the child in the land
of promise. But Abraham's delay also delayed the plan of God
for their life.

God is waiting on us, so we can drop off some stuff and
some people in our lives, in order for Him to move us into
our encounter with our destiny. The delay is not on the part
of God or heaven because God is ever ready. The delay is with
us because we are dragging our feet to move beyond our past.
"For *THEY* went with *THEM*." It is interesting, isn't it? If
you ever want to come into dominion with God, you need to
identify who the "*THEM*" are in your life and to get rid of the
"*THEM*."

The Cause of Abraham's Instability

Notice that God did not appear unto Abraham again until his father Terah died in Charran, and then as soon as Terah died, God said to Abraham, "Remember I told you to leave your father's house and your kindred." So now Abraham decided to continue his journey towards Canaan but then again, he took with him his nephew Lot, which was another big mistake on the part of Abraham. So watch what happens after that. When they got to the land of Canaan, and Abraham began to move around and walk through the land, for some reason, Abraham could not settle. Notice in Genesis 13, that he moved to **Sichem**, and built an altar, and moved to the **plains of Moreh**, and then moved himself again to **Bethel** and there again built an altar. He just could not settle, and the reason why he could not settle was because he still had his nephew Lot with him on the journey. Hence there was conflict between his past and his present.

....

Conflict is when you are still thinking according to the order of your past mindset but hear a present word from God.

....

In order for you to overcome that conflict, you have to battle it within yourself, whether to yield to your old mindset or to go in the direction of a renewal of mind. This is exactly like the saying of Jesus that, *"You cannot put new wine into an old bottle."*

You've got to make a firm decision not to take your past into your present or else you will either miss or delay your encounter with God. Abraham was where he was supposed to be, but there was no stability, because he had people who were not supposed to be with him on the journey. Many people have the same problem. They are where they're supposed to be, but they have around them some people who are not supposed to be with them.

Like Abraham, until they get rid of all those people, God's agenda will be delayed in their lives. That is why, although many people have surrendered their lives to Christ and they are in Church, which is a good thing, they still have some things or some people from their past who are pulling them down spiritually. That's why some people have been in Church for so many years and yet cannot grow spiritually.

Whenever you take your past with you into your future, it will create conflict in your present.

I will prove this saying to you from **Genesis 13:5-7**. *"And Lot also, which went with Abram, had flocks, and herds, and tents. [6] And the land was not able to bear them, that they might dwell together: for their substance was great, so that they could not dwell together. [7] And there was a strife between the herdsmen of Abram's cattle and the herdsmen of Lot's cattle: and the Canaanite and the Perizzite dwelled then in the land.*

Verse 7 of the above passage says, *[7] **And there was a strife between the herdsmen of Abram's cattle and the herdsmen of Lot's cattle:***

That's what happens when you try to take your relative past into your future. It's going to end up in conflict. So again, and just like before, God had to pull away from Abraham whiles Lot was still with him until Lot was separated from Him after the conflict arose. How did I know this? Let us see what Genesis Chapter 13 says about this.

> ***"And the Lord said unto Abram, after that Lot was separated from him, Lift up now thine eyes, and look from the place where thou art northward, and southward, and eastward, and westward: [15] For all the land which thou seest, to thee will I give it, and to thy seed forever. [16] And I will make thy seed as the dust of the earth: so that if a man can number the dust of the earth, then shall thy seed also be numbered. [17] Arise, walk through the land in the length of it and in the breadth of it, for I will give it unto thee."*** (Gen. 13; 14-17)

See how the verse begins, ***"And the Lord said unto Abram, after that Lot was separated from him . . . "***

Notice that it was only after Terah was gone and Lot was also gone away from Abraham that God gave him the permission to walk through the land and to possess it. You cannot be ready to walk through the land and to possess your possessions until you part with your past and get rid of the people in your life who shouldn't be there.

The fact that God had to wait for both Terah and Lot to be separated from Abraham before he gave Abraham permission to walk through the land and to possess it, provides a message for every one of us to learn, because at times when God opens a door, it is not always meant for you to go through. At times when God opens a door, it is for the people who are around you who are not supposed to be with you, to go through. Immediately after they go through those opened doors, God may quickly shut the door behind them.

So, God opens a door before Lot and Lot was so much enticed by the greener plains of Sodom, and he quickly moved towards the land of Sodom together with his herdsman. Watch what happens next. God then shuts the door behind Lot, and gave Abraham the fullness of the blessing he had promised to give him the first time He appeared and spoke to Abraham. And look at what that promise entails, according to **Genesis 13:14-17, *"From the northward, and southward, and eastward, and westward: [15] For all the land which thou seest, to thee will I give it, and to thy seed forever. [16] And I will make thy seed as the dust of the earth: so that if a man can number the dust of the earth, then shall thy seed also be numbered. [17] Arise, walk through the land in the length of it and in the breadth of it, for I will give it unto thee."***

Therefore, quit rushing to go through every door that you see opened and begin to seek God for guidance. Ask which doors he would want you to walk through because not every opened door is an opportunity and not everything that is good, is the right thing to do. Remember, other doors are opened by God for you, and can lead you to those who will make your journey with you as your dearest friends.

'Food-For-Thought'

Worksheet for Chapter 7

Words of Wisdom

1. You have realized that you made a lot of mistakes and wrong choices in the past. How do you move beyond that?

   i. Living with your "past" in your "present" can create a conflict in your "future."

2. How then must I handle my past?

   i. Learn to forgive your past as if it is a person and begin to see and move beyond it.

3. The greatest enemy of your future is when you allow either the successes or failures of your past to stand in the way of your future.

4. How then do I handle my successes and failures?

   i. Convert your successes into stepping stones towards greater achievement.

   ii. Convert your failures into lessons learned in order not to repeat and retard your future progress.